WHEN POLICE KILL

When Police Kill

POLICE USE OF FORCE IN
MONTREAL AND TORONTO

Gabriella Pedicelli

Véhicule Press

Véhicule Press gratefully acknowledges the support of
The Canada Council for the Arts for its publishing program.

Cover art and design: J.W. Stewart
Cover imaging: André Jacob
Printing: AGMV-Marquis Inc.

CANADIAN CATALOGUING IN PUBLICATION DATA

Pedicelli, Gabriella
When police kill : police use of force
in Montreal and Toronto

Inclues bibliographical references.

1. Police shootings–Ontario–Toronto. 2. Police
shootings–Quebec–Montréal. 3. Police misconduct–
Ontario–Toronto. 4. Police misconduct–Quebec
(Province)–Montréal. 5. Discrimination in criminal
justice administration–Ontario–Toronto.
6. Discrimination in criminal justice administration–
Quebec (Province)–Montréal. I. Title.

HV8158.P43 1998   363.2'32   C98-900199-7

Véhicule Press
P.O.B. 125, Place du Parc Station
Montreal, Quebec H2W 2M9

http://www.cam.org/~vpress

DISTRIBUTED BY GENERAL DISTRIBUTION SERVICES

Printed in Canada on alkaline paper.

Contents

Preface

Due to limited accessibility to official government sources, most of the information used to analyze deaths caused by the police was collected from the media, primarily newspapers. Although the Access to Information Act is intended to help the public obtain of official information, it is not user friendly. For example, neither government nor police sources could provide a listing of police-inflicted deaths because such a listing was not compiled by government sources. The de-contextualized nature and contextualized piece-meal presentation in the media means that it alone cannot be relied upon to present this issue of police use of force accurately.

In the following research, news sources were used to collect information about incidents in Montreal and Toronto and to compile a chronological listing of deaths caused by police between 1987 and 1993 in these cities. Neither city administration could provide such information. Newspapers were also used to collect information to connect details concerning the controversies resulting from these incidents and to develop a more complete picture. My intention has been to create a bridge for the inadequate information disseminated through the media and official sources by placing it in context.

The chapter dealing with the media examines how and in what manner stories regarding crime were presented in mainstream papers. The first section discusses a three-part series in the *Globe & Mail* which focussed on implicating Jamaicans as the primary perpetrators of black crime in Toronto.

In the second section, all of the articles which appeared in the Montreal *Gazette* in June 1995 which concentrated on the police were analyzed. This research was undertaken to evaluate and demonstrate how media can choose and disseminate information. The focus of the research was intentionally centred on newspaper crime reporting and editorials that had the police as its subject.

Introduction

Between 1987 and 1993 there were many deaths under questionable circumstances caused by the police in Montreal and Toronto. This provoked much public controversy regarding police abuse. Many citizens are fearful of the police who, they fear, can no longer be relied on to serve and protect. It is as a consequence of these conflicts that I have become passionately concerned with the issues surrounding the police, and more specifically, the legitimacy of their mandate which permits the use of deadly force and killings.

I developed these sentiments towards the police as a young adult. In my last year of high school I decided that I wanted to become a police officer. Why? It may have been that I did not know what I wanted to do, and initially the police technology program seemed to be interesting. In my mind I believed that I was not going to be just any cop; not the cops my friends and I were constantly confronting as teenagers, not the ones who emptied our beer out into the sewer when we drank in the park, or who periodically cornered us and wrote down our names and addresses in their notebooks, or who would watch the pool hall where we hung out from across the street just to intimidate us. I was going to be a good cop, one who understood what it was like to be intimidated and harassed needlessly. And so there it was—I had established the false ideal that I would be different from the other officers and that I could make a positive difference. I now realize it was naive and wishful thinking.

In September 1985 I began the police technology program at John Abbott College in Montreal and breezed through. Not that this was difficult since the program consisted of memorizing verbatim the various lists of procedures, rules, regulations and the all important steps and phases. Knowledge was reduced to lists and step-by-step processes. I cannot recall any police course which attempted to direct students to deal with the public compassionately, or to sensitize them to cultural and economic diversities. It was at this stage that my not so rude awakening occurred, due to the course content, the professors' dogmatic attitudes, and students' eagerness to apprehend criminals. I came to the realization that it would be impossible for me to be any different from the officers whom I had encountered as an adolescent. There could be only two possible outcomes; either I would eventually be fired from the force because of my inability to follow the rules and regulations, or I would be assimilated into the policing culture and become one of them. It was the thought of becoming one of them which caused me to abandon policing.

Once I successfully completed the three year college program, I decided to follow through on the ten week training at the Nicolet police academy. Why? At that point I knew that I no longer wanted to become a police officer but felt that it would be useful to attend to understand what the practical training involved. Although the three years I spent at the college and at the training academy could, at first glance, be considered a waste of time, I learned a tremendous amount concerning the policing institution and the way it really functions. Cowboy attitudes, from both the instructors and the cadets, were more pronounced at the academy than at the college. The tightly structured military lifestyle only reaffirmed the authoritarian nature of policing. Students who stepped outside the military-style boundaries received negative sanctions. After twelve sanctions a student is expelled; I managed to receive eleven. They were given to me for, among other things, not sufficiently shining my shoes, neglecting to wear my name tag, having a crease in my shirt, having a hair in my sink, having a hair rest on my shirt collar, and having a thumb print on my hat visor. We were only taught the crime fighting model of policing, of firearms training, high speed chases, self-defence, search and seizure, handcuffing, properly stopping vehicles, and safety measures when answering calls.

When an officer kills it is the ultimate manifestation of police power. I was interested in studying these killings, especially in relation to police accountability. I have come to understand police power as an immense and insurmountable entity which theoretically exists to protect but which may ultimately oppress. The purpose of this book is to inform. Since information regarding police abuses is not readily accessible using either the police system or the media, I have compiled the information in a concise and inclusive form to be used as a tool and resource guide to promote public awareness about, and action against, these injustices. It is important for people to act to change the status quo of police violence in our communities. The material here is basic to understanding how and why that violence occurs and is publicly sanctioned.

The book begins by discussing the false premises of policing, and traces its inception in England, the United States and Canada. The constraints placed on police officers in the Criminal Code of Canada concerning the use of force, as well as police discretion which can ultimately lead to certain groups being negatively targeted by the police, are then enumerated. The role of the media in providing information to the public regarding situations of police abuse is examined. Specific cases involving deaths caused by the police in Montreal and Toronto between 1987 and 1993 are discussed, and are followed by an in-depth analysis of the Allan Gosset case. The organizational changes implemented by police institutions in Ontario and Quebec as a result of the killings and an evaluation of their effectiveness are outlined. The conclusion presents options for citizen-initiated action designed to change the current situation.

> To be governed, is to be, at every operation, at every transaction, with every movement, noted, registered, counted, given a fixed rate, stamped, measured, assessed, licensed, certified, authorized, given tentative approval, reprimanded, impeded, discharged, set straight, corrected. It is, under the pretext of public purposes, and in the name of the general interest, to be placed under requisition, made use of, held at ransom, exploited, subjected to monopolies, exposed to extortion, squeezed, baffled, robbed; then, at the least resistance, at the first word of complaint, suppressed, fined, vilified, harassed, hunted down, bullied, bludgeoned, disarmed, garroted, imprisoned, shot, machine gunned, judged, sentenced, transported, sacrificed, sold, betrayed, and to crown it all, mocked, ridiculed, insulted, dishonoured. That's government, that's its justice, that's its morality!

—Proudhon

CHAPTER ONE

The False Premise
of Policing

The police are viewed as a necessary institution of control in contemporary societies. Most people accept this belief whole-heartedly and without question. In fact, we willingly relinquish control to the police, and most members of society want to be governed and policed. Why do people accept the existence of the police institution as a control agency which surveys, regulates, and monitors citizens? There are three interconnected false assumptions which dominate thinking and aid in maintaining police legitimacy. This accepted false legitimacy largely explains the public acceptance of intrusive front-line police officers.

The first false assumption about policing is its perception as a natural and inevitable institution within any society. State power, specifically police authority, is considered by most to be a natural, as opposed to an instilled, process which is required to maintain social order. The second assumption is the false ideal of neutrality. The police are regarded as the arm of the state whose primary function is enforcing social discipline and maintaining order. Generally, most people view the state as neutral, that all members of society are treated without prejudice, fairly and equally. Since the police are the front-line workers, they are also perceived and accepted as legitimate. The presupposition is that since the police are an extension of the state they ascribe to its standards of neutrality and fairness. They are considered to be neutral arbitrators of the law of fair and equal treatment for all, which is at the heart of their mandate. The final assumption contributing to police legitimacy arises from the prima facie assumption that force and authority are necessary to maintain control and conformity within any society. We are led to believe that without this aspect of present day policing, society and, more specifically, our communities, will be plagued with disorder and eventual chaos. It remains inconceivable to many that an orderly society might exist without codified rules which require police enforcement. Most people believe that without rules society cannot exist. As a result, state control, expressed through policing, presents itself as a necessity in which the exercise of power by the few over the many is unquestionably legitimate. Submission to authority is deemed necessary to achieve and maintain social stability. The police become a tool to coerce individuals into submission in the name of order. It is through these three assumptions and their acceptance by the public that the police are legitimized.

In order to demonstrate the falsity of these assumptions it is important to consider the development of professional institutionalized policing in modern times. From their inception, policing organizations were established for reasons other than the maintenance of social order. Present day policing functions have evolved with these biases as an integral component. The rationalization for the development of professional policing in Britain in the 1820s, in the United States in 1845, and Canada in 1873 will be discussed. This will demonstrate that professional policing was not established to serve all members of society equally, rather that policing emerged from a need to control certain segments of the population to encourage and protect industrial development.

BRITAIN

Modern professional policing began in Britain in the 1820s. Its inception has been attributed to a need for increased control over the working classes to maintain the interests of the ruling classes. The following quote is revealing, "Because the English Bourgeois finds himself reproduced in his law, as he does in his God, the policeman's truncheon... has for him a wonderfully soothing power. But for the workman quite otherwise!"[1] Why was a new form of policing considered necessary at that time? Industrialization and subsequent urbanization created a need for a submissive and passive work force which the police would be able to control. A pattern of extreme class division between industrialists and workers developed which had not previously existed. The rapid growth of cities caused a more visible segregation of the classes, which exacerbated worker hostility and dislocation. Individuals who rebelled against the capitalist order were defined as socially undisciplined. The poor who flooded into the cities became defined as the dangerous classes requiring the control of an organized police force. Worker resistance to unhealthy and dangerous work conditions was perceived as a crime. This validated the need for professional police to combat the increase in a newly defined criminality. [2]

As a part of the development of capitalism and the industrial revolution, private and public lives became more regimented to adapt to the conditions of mass production.[3] The police became the regulators of both private and working life. Those who benefited from the new police institutions were the property owners whose interests were being protected. The central function of the police, as an instrument of enforcement for the economic and political elite of the time, was to control and pacify the working classes into submission to the capitalist order.

THE UNITED STATES

The earliest form of non-professional policing in the United States was the Southern slave patrols. Because black slaves were the principal labourers in the South throughout the eighteenth and nineteenth centuries, the patrols were necessary to protect the land owners' property rights to their slaves. Discipline was maintained by whipping any slave attempting to escape, riot or revolt against the established order.[4] In the American North and West the suppression of Native Americans became a catalyst for non-professional policing. Indigenous peoples were a threat to the colonial economy because their territories included desirable, resources-rich land. Militias were created to facilitate the acquisition of Native land, most often by force, for English settlers.[5]

The initial need for policing evolved out of issues of slavery, racism and colonialist conquests; institutionalized policing came about to control working class unrest resulting from rapid industrial expansion and urbanization, as had happened in Britain two decades earlier. The first modern American professional police force was established in New York in 1845 to control conflicts created by industrialization. These forces were larger and better armed than non-professional militias. The process of industrialization, beginning in the 1830s and lasting through the Civil War, led to the depression of wages and a demand for unskilled, rather than skilled, workers. As a result, class struggles intensified. This led to active worker resistance against exploitation which included labour strikes, unions, the destruction of production machinery, food riots and radical political organizing, which was defined as criminal activity by the ruling class. Historical evidence indicates that workers fought against the creation of a police institution which was the result of a determined effort by those in power to maintain capitalism while controlling the workers. Police forces were re-organized specifically to deal effectively with worker resistance to industrial development.[6]

<u>CANADA</u>

In Canada, the North West Mounted Police (NWMP) was created in 1873 (it is now the Royal Canadian Mounted Police) with a different motivation. Although this was not the first professional police force in Canada, its reputation makes it important. In 1869, as a result of Confederation, arrangements were made between the government of Great Britain and the directors of the Hudson's Bay Company to relinquish Rupert's Land, which was inhabited by Métis and the First Nations, to the Canadian federal government; as well as to confederate British Columbia. The confederation of British Columbia was predicated on the construction of a trans-continental railway. The Canadian government needed to control passage to the Pacific for any such project to succeed. The railway would then be used to encourage immigration and thus create a profitable market for the manufactured goods of central Canada. It would also make the vast resources of the west accessible for exploration and exploitation. The NWMP was used to seize resource-rich Métis land and transfer control and effective ownership to the federal government. This semi-military police force was created to control Métis resistance as well as potential native allies farther west who also revolted against the forceable take-over of their land by the Canadian government. The federal government feared a war waged by the Métis and natives against white settlers.[7] The belief was that the NWMP would civilize the wild, bar-baric, heathen Indians. The mission was violently and enthusiastically carried out by its racist officers.

In 1885 simmering Métis resentments about unaddressed grievances flared into rebellion in Saskatchewan. These grievances stemmed from government policy mandating the NWMP to tame Indian tribes, move them to reserves and acquire their land. The native way of life would be destroyed and the native problem would cease to exist. The NWMP, along with the military, actively participated in the suppression of this rebellion and were instrumental in punishing the rebels. Approximately 18 Métis and 30 Indians were incarcerated; Métis leader Louis Riel and eight Indians were executed. As a deterrent to similar rebellions, Natives from nearby reserves were encouraged to attend the public executions of the eight Indians at the NWMP stockade at Battleford. The following passage, taken from Caroline and Lorne Brown's, *An Unauthorized History of the RCMP*, is a description of the executions:

> As the hour drew near, weird chanting arose from the direction of the Indian camp, and as one by one the condemned were conducted from the barracks the impressive dirge grew louder. Among those about to die there was little evidence of mental agitation; several joked openly and chatted casually. The shackles they had worn were removed, but their arms were pinioned. Each walked between and was preceded and followed by Mounted Police constables. They were soon on the scaffold, each beneath a dangling rope. But before the eight ropes were adjusted and black caps drawn over eight shaven heads, all were told they could speak for ten minutes. Only Ikta and Little Bear availed themselves of the privilege, both shouting defiance. Others uttered a few high pitched war cries or sang their weird lamentations. Wandering Spirit was completely resigned and undemonstrative. Then Hodson spoke, silence fell and the bolt was drawn.
>
> All died instantly. The bodies were hurried away in rough pine boxes and committed to a common grave on the hillside below the barracks.
>
> The days of the scalping knife and war clubs were definitely in the past.[8]

Louis Riel was accused and convicted of committing high treason against the Canadian government and was hanged on November 16, 1885.[9]

The brief history of policing in the three countries provokes questions about the legitimacy of the policing system by demonstrating that its professional form came about only at the middle of the 19th century. From the beginning it protected the interests of a specific powerful segment of the population and their capitalist interests. Historically the primary function of the police has been to protect the status quo of wealth and well-being of those who benefit most from an economy based on profit and accumulation of private property. The institution of policing was created in response to working class opposition to oppressive working and living conditions in developing industrial centres. The police were not created to serve all of society or all the people, but to serve some at the expense of others.

The police institution represents, and has always represented, the repressive aspect of the state because it has been used to control segments of the population which threaten or challenge the prevailing dominant economic and political structure. Since it has never been neutral or for the good of the collectivity, it cannot be assumed that it is so today. Remnants of its origins are still visible in present-day police activities which target the powerless in society—often visible minorities and the poor.

The 'Legitimate' Use of Force

Every year there is a memorial service in Ottawa for Canadian police officers killed in the line of duty. And every year thousands of officers from across Canada congregate to pay their respects and remember their fallen confreres. The 1985 service included a Bible reading from the book of John, Chapter XV; "Jesus said to his disciples: 'if the world hates you, remember that it hated me before you. If you belonged to the world, the world would love you as its own; but because you do not belong to the world, because my choice withdrew you from the world, therefore the world hates you.'" Does[10] this reading imply that police officers have been anointed by God to do His work on earth and have been ordained as modern day disciples? Perhaps it is this false premise which is used to validate the policing institution, a premise which assumes that the police are needed to protect us from ourselves, at which point the public/police relationship becomes adversarial. The commonly held view of policing presupposes that the police see the world more clearly than the rest of society and therefore have the right to exercise power over it. Because of this accepted superiority, they have the right to act outside accepted norms and use physical force in the commission of their duties. As with the military, the police engage in more acts of coercion than most other government agencies, the most controversial of which takes the form of physical violence which may be fatal to its victims. In fact, the mandate to use force, including deadly force, stands at the core of the police raison d'être and is perceived as a normal and acceptable aspect of policing. It is one of the few organizations whose mandate allows for the legally sanctioned killing of people. Policing is defined by the potential for violence which it possesses and requires to defend society against wrong-doers.[11] The major problem which this coercion allows is that, depending on how it is exercised, this power permits the police to not act on behalf of the people they are meant to serve. Instead, the lines of fair and equal treatment become blurred. It can be argued that the police are a tool to force citizens into submission.

The adversarial relationship which exists between the police and the community is most clearly visible in the extreme cases of killings by police. A shooting is the most dramatic event in the professional life of a police officer because, resembling a Greek morality play, it represents the ultimate confrontation between good and evil. Shootings by police officers will almost always appear justified to the officers, as well as to the state, regardless of circumstance. Officers involved in shootings often make use of the policing institution's coping mechanisms which absolve them of any blame for wrongdoing. They adopt techniques of neutralization which both justify the killing of an individual and legitimize their adherence to the training and regulations of the police force. The techniques involve accepting stereotypes associated with specific characteristics of an individual, such as race, sex, age, or style of dress. Such a justification occurs when officers interpret race as a cause of crime. Another neutralizing technique involves the belief that justice is rarely rightfully served because so many guilty individuals are not punished, and as such, an extreme punishment is better than none.[12]

When lethal or near-lethal force is used, officers often legitimize their response by explaining it as a normal reaction to an extreme situation. However, this normal reaction is a result of their training. Officers are taught that emphasis should be on the crime-fighting model of policing, with apprehension as the most important task, and they therefore adopt the role of law enforcers.[13] The police academy teaches its officers to deal with criminals as individual wrong-doers, without considering the circumstances of the particular situation or the social context in which the alleged crimes take place. The criminal is seen as a bad apple needing restraint and correction to be set right and in step with the rest of society.

Research in both the United States and Canada demonstrates that the police are more prone to use force when dealing with visible minorities and the poor— reflecting the racial bias of the policing institution and Criminal Justice System as a whole.[14] Police use of force against these groups may then be attributed to the structural imperatives of a society. Since, in theory, inequality is unnatural within a democratic society founded on freedom and equality, it can only be maintained by force, resulting in one interpretation of law for the rich and another for the poor. Increased levels of state coercion are visible in areas where inequality is most pronounced. Not only are the members of these groups more likely to be harassed by police, they are also less likely to succeed in redressing problems with the police through complaints. Data about American police forces suggests that race and ethnicity are important factors in determining the outcome of complaints, even though these complaints have often involved serious allegations of assault and brutality.[15] A relationship exists between police power and control and the need to maintain respect for their authority. Violence against visible minorities, primarily blacks and hispanics, occurs most often when these groups demonstrate a lack of respect towards the police. However, this attitude is often the result of routine mistreatment by the police. Because of their actions the police are a symbol of all that is hated. It is a vicious cycle of police mistreatment of certain groups leading to distrust and a lack of respect which ultimately results in further mistreatment.

Most police killings involve the use of firearms. The police justify carrying guns by pointing out that many of the individuals they deal with have guns. But police officers are highly trained in the use of firearms, are familiar with them, and inspect and maintain their weapons and ammunition, while citizens often do not. Citizens frequently have inoperative and inappropriate weapons which are used improperly.[16] The police are usually at an advantage over their adversaries with regard to the use of their firearms. A study conducted about the police use of deadly force in Canada concluded that Canadian police officers use their guns much less frequently than American officers but that shooting incidents are much less regulated and officers are less likely to be convicted of any wrong-doing involving the use of force.[17] Police discretionary powers in Canada are greater while their accountability is lower. Even when the legitimacy of the use of force is challenged, most police organizations limit the scope of any external review.

Because the above assumptions are accepted as legitimate by society, physical force is assumed to be a necessary aspect for the successful execution of police duties. It is a vital part of their mandate. Research indicates that the police use of force is illegitimately used against particular segments of society which are considered to be a threat.

CHAPTER TWO

The Freedom to Abuse

In order to understand the limits placed on Canadian police forces regarding the use of force, the laws as defined in the Criminal Code which apply to Canadian police officers will be described. A general discussion about the use of language is important here because it is one of the most effective tools contributing to public acquiescence to the state. Language use can discourage alternative or marginal ways of thinking and behaving.[1] The state can maintain its coercive power over individuals only when their ability to think and to make distinctions between ideas is defined by state-sanctioned language and ideology. The terminology used in the Criminal Code of Canada is designed to shape specific patterns of thinking which accommodate and compliment the status quo of no police accountability. Furthermore, due to the Code's lack of clear-cut guidelines officers, by default, have wide discretionary powers regarding the use of force. The Criminal Code does, however, succeed in creating the illusion that limits do exist.

There is a distinction made between 'use' and 'abuse' of force within the policing organization and in the Criminal Justice System as a whole. A brief comment about use and abuse demonstrates the maintenance of police legitimacy for the use of physical force. The terms use and abuse, as binary opposites, must be questioned since they ultimately distort our thinking. Their use illustrates how accepted meanings are created and how these meanings, when defined as truth, suppress alternative meanings. In the present case, their use serves to create a patterned self-validating distinction. Abuse of deadly force assumes that there is a legitimate use of deadly force. *Words can lose all meaning when use becomes legitimized through the imposed term of abuse.* Police officers become executioners, allowed to kill without proof of the victim's guilt. In no other occupation, apart from soldiers during war, are individuals granted a license to kill. Since police officers are considered to be neutral law enforcers, they are deemed qualified to determine when force is necessary in the commission of their duties.

George Orwell, in 1984, discussed 'Controltalk.' This device, rather than decreasing language, increases vocabulary in an attempt to create a language for punishment[2] In the sections of the Criminal Code applying to police use of force, there are key phrases which grant the police the power to impose physical punishment and, sometimes, to kill. It is important to assess the terminology used in the Criminal Code of Canada and the manner in which it is interpreted. An examination of the key phrases in the Code sections within the context of use of force helps to define the extent of the legal limitations imposed on the police, the clarity of these prescribed limitations, and, more importantly, the degree of discretion allowed to police officers as a result. It is a given that policing organizations allow wide discretionary powers to front-line officers in every facet of police work. From the initial communication centre where calls from the public are screened, to whether or not to arrest or to use force, the lowest ranking police officers are granted the power to make critical decisions. The extent of these discretionary powers, as well as the extent of accountability when they are abused, must be determined.

There are five sections of the Criminal Code of Canada (S.25(1), 25(3), 25(4), 26 and 27) which apply specifically to police officers and the use or abuse of force. Use and abuse is defined in Section 25 (1), 'Protection of Persons Acting Under Authority,' a general provision which allows police officers the right, when acting on reasonable and probable grounds, to use 'as much force as necessary' in the commission of their duties.[3] The two key concepts of 'reasonable grounds', and 'as much force as necessary' in this section afford the police a wide range of discretionary powers. As in a number of the following sections, and in law in general, separating use from abuse is based on the 'reasonable man' standard, the defined objective standard prescribed by law. This standard adheres to two precepts. Officers must subjectively have reasonable and probable grounds for their actions; and those grounds must be justifiable from an objective point of view— that a 'reasonable' person, placed in the officer's position must be able to conclude that there were sufficient grounds for the action.[4] However, depending on the individual, the definition of reasonable will differ, making it impossible to achieve a standard of collective objectivity. The standard becomes an unrealistic ideal which may not be judged in the same manner, especially between police officers and civilians. Who actually determines what is reasonable? When an action is called into question, it is the arbiter of facts, judge or jury, who ultimately decides what is reasonable to them, thus breaking down the apparently objective standard. Individuals who are required to place themselves in the position of the implicated officer, because of their inexperience and lack of training in the area of policing, are likely to agree with the officer's decision. Because jurors often give police officers this benefit of the doubt, officers are rarely found guilty of criminal charges involving an excessive use of force.

This section of the Criminal Code also allows a broad definition of 'as much force as necessary;' it is unclear whether the phrase is intended to include lethal and near-lethal use of force. It is vague and does not prescribe clear guidelines for police officers beyond individual judgement. Who determines how much force was actually necessary in a given situation after the fact? Many civilians and judges will, once again, defer to the judgement of police officers in determining what is required in the execution of their duties because of their specific training and position as experts in the area of policing.

Sub-Section 25 (3)- 'When Not Protected,' limits the use of lethal and near-lethal force to situations where it is required to preserve the life of the officer or a citizen when a direct and immediate threat is posed. If the use of force leads to death, as long as it has been applied to preserve a life, it is justified.[5]

This limit on the use of lethal or near lethal force is broadened in section 25(4), 'The Fleeing Felon Provision.' Prior to 1994 this section stated that police officers, while arresting a person, were justified in using 'as much force as necessary' if that person attempted to escape or flee, unless the escape could have been prevented in a less violent manner. Although the section stipulates that an escape must, if possible, be prevented in another manner, the focus is on preventing the escape at any cost, regardless of whether an imposed threat to the officer's life or anyone else's exists. There has been controversy concerning its use; in several cases where individuals were killed the police justified their action by claiming that the victim was fleeing an arrest at the time, even though there was no threat to anyone's life. Extensive media attention was given to two young black men, Anthony Griffin in Montreal in 1987 and Michael Wade Lawson in Toronto in 1988, who were both shot and killed under questionable circumstances. Michael Lawson was shot in the back, while Anthony Griffin was shot in the forehead after he had obeyed the officer's order to halt. Both men were later discovered to have been unarmed, they were not posing any immediate danger to the officers or other individuals. They were killed because they had attempted to flee, which was sufficient reason to exonerate the officers involved of any criminal responsibility.

As a result of black community outrage, in February 1994 a bill was introduced to amend the 'fleeing felon' provision of the Criminal Code. The new bill attempted to clarify and restrict when police officers might legitimately use force which could cause death to prevent a suspect from fleeing. However, the section remained unchanged except for the insertion of a preservation of life element. This limited the use of lethal force in a fleeing suspect situation to the presence of the threat of immediate or future death or grievous bodily harm.[6]

It would appear that an attempt was made to limit the use of police lethal or near-lethal force in a fleeing suspect situation. Closer inspection confirms that the amendment further loosened restrictions by allowing force to be used in the absence of any immediate danger by introducing the concept of a 'future danger.' By permitting the use of lethal or near-lethal force where the belief in a possible future danger exists permits enormous leeway for the police officer. In addition, it allows an officer a wide variety of justifications to legitimize the course of action taken if that action is later questioned. There is no stipulation about what this future projection of danger must be based on, or how it will later be measured in court. This extra clause does not define what 'future danger' encompasses, or how it is assessed, and ultimately relies on the reasonable belief of the police officer involved. Since evaluation of the situation will only occur after the fact, there are endless justifications which the officer might employ in defending the use of the extreme force, especially when there are no witnesses. The validity of the amendment must be questioned. In practice is additional clause has not limited police use of lethal or near-lethal force to immediate preservation of life, and it is inadequate to address public concerns. The amendment would not have changed the outcome of either the Griffin or Lawson case because, when they were killed, the officers had no way of knowing whether or not they were armed.

As in its earlier form, the amended section also stipulates that lethal or near-lethal force can only be used if the escape can not be prevented in a less violent manner. Once again, it requires a trained police officer's judgement in the specific situation. The police officer, as an expert, is viewed as more qualified to determine what action is necessary to prevent an escape. It is extremely difficult to determine, after the fact, whether a less violent course of action would have sufficed.

The Canadian Association of Chiefs of Police, which represents 35,000 police officers across the country, did not support the amendment because they believed that it would encourage suspects to flee unimpeded.[7] This denial of support is indicative of the policing organization's lack of initiative in curbing on-going abuses, and demonstrates that their main priority is apprehension at any cost. The attitude is that it is better for an individual to be killed than to be allowed to escape justice—even for a trivial matter such as failing to pay a cab fare, as was the case with Anthony Griffin.

Section 26, 'Excessive Force', of the Code states that police officers who act outside the prescribed provisions of the Code's earlier sections may be held criminally responsible for their actions.[8] The broadness of the limits makes it difficult to prove beyond a reasonable doubt whether or not any action taken by an officer is outside the stipulated parameters.

Section 27, 'Use of Force to Prevent Commission of Offence', states that an officer may use as much force as is reasonably necessary to prevent anything that she or he reasonably believes would be an offence causing immediate and serious injury to persons or property.[9] Unlike Section 25(1), Section 27 places no limits on the use of lethal force; any level of force is acceptable to prevent an offence which threatens persons or property. It widens the scope of the legitimate use of lethal force to such an extent that the value of property is equated with the value of a human life. To further blur the restrictions, the Section states that an actual offence need not be in the process of being committed. Force may be used so long as the police officer reasonably believes that an offence is in the process of being committed, even if after the fact it is discovered to have been unfounded. What is required is the police officer's reasonable belief. An important case where this section applies is that of Marcellus François. In 1991 Marcellus François, a 24 year old black man, was shot and killed in his car in Montreal by the Tactical Squad when they allegedly mistook him for an armed attempted-murder suspect; even though the physical descriptions of François and the suspect were completely different. Marcellus had short hair, was five foot seven and weighed 130 pounds, while the suspect had knee-length braids, was six feet tall and weighed 160 pounds. When the implicated officers were tried in court, they were exonerated of any criminal responsibility. The court's conclusion that this action was reasonably based questions the validity of the prescribed standard of collective objectivity previously discussed. It is unlikely that a reasonable individual placed in the position of the implicated officers would have mistaken François for the suspect, or reacted in the same manner and executed the same course of action. If the police were not responsible in the Marcellus François case where there was an obvious abuse of force, it is unlikely that they will ever be held accountable.

The legislative sections of the Criminal Code are based on an impossible standard of objectivity and impartiality. The lack of clarity and the vagueness of the specific sections pertaining to the allowable use of force obliges police officers to rely on individual discretion in determining how and when laws should be enforced. The laws which define the distinctions between use and abuse of force, as in all areas of law, do not, and cannot, outline clear-cut guidelines encompassing every possible situation a police officer might encounter. Much of the actual decision-making is discretionary, falling into the hands of the individual front-line officer involved in a particular situation.

Police discretionary powers are often legitimized on this inadequacy and ambiguity within the law. The law is presented as the mechanism which confines and controls police abuse of force; in reality it fails to do so and opens the way for police discretion. Police discretion must not be viewed in light of the failure of the law to restrict courses of action, but as an unregulated tool which sets the precise, sought out standards of conduct.

This leads to specific segments of society being targeted, irrespective of the law. The prescribed informal standards set within the policing institution compliment the status quo. Allowing police officers such wide discretionary powers, especially in the area of physical force, permits uncontrollable abuses of power.

Uniformity in decision-making concerning discretionary decisions and power is impossible because of the differing judgements and experiences of individual officers.[10] This assertion is partly true since determining the correct course of action in a given circumstance is based on the officer's individual and personal evaluation, which is often grounded in systemic stereotypes based on expected behaviour.[11] These discretionary abuses, which are based on stereotypes, are rooted at the organizational level and include internal operating norms and police socialization. The expected behaviour of an individual is defined according to an informal set of rules among police officers which are based on this labelling process. An officer, when encountering a specific individual, will assess the level of danger according to these stereotypic labels which have been informally pre-established within the policing collective. As a result, certain members of the population will be targeted as deserving special attention, based on specific criteria outlined by police officers, including race, appearance, age and geographical area. A young black man living in an urban low-income housing project will be defined as dangerous, and is therefore considered dangerous by most officers. This will, in turn, affect any confrontation. This process creates the perception that there is a dangerous class of individuals, regardless of any real threat to police officers or society.

Vast discretionary powers expand the police role to include policing, prosecution, as well as judge and jury. By using force, front-line officers may also become executioners. They have been granted the power to kill—before the suspect has been found guilty in a court of law of the alleged crime she or he might have been accused of committing.

CHAPTER THREE

A Pawn in the Game

The Mass Media

The mass media is of great importance because of the crucial role it plays in informing the public about police abuses, influencing public opinion, and keeping controversy alive. As a result, these institutions have a responsibility to their audience. An enormous amount of power is vested in the mainstream media because they have the power to shape public awareness. It is important to assess the manner in which the media choose to present controversial police conduct to determine whether they promote police legitimacy or challenge it.

The mass media disseminates information, knowledge, values and images regarding the world we live in which are consistent with the dominant value system.[1] Crime becomes news because, as a negative thing, it reinforces the common value system created by the social structure which distinguishes between right and wrong. The mass media is a crucial player in defining particular concepts of crime to society. Since the media and their messages are structured within this framework of power, apparently objective and impartial news coverage must be questioned because of bias in the selection and presentation of reports. The alleged balance of opinions in news stories is, in fact, also biased because alternative and opposing definitions are rarely provided.

It has been argued that journalists have a social responsibility to disseminate knowledge to an audience which cannot obtain information concerning events occurring beyond their immediate environment.[2] This knowledge, as it is presented, is neither neutral nor objective. It is a representation of the world, biased in favour of the views and the agendas of the people responsible for creating it. The circulation and dissemination of this knowledge is not necessarily perceived as a social responsibility by journalists, but is instead an act which attempts to mask contradictions and inequalities. The news media's power rests in its ability to construct and circulate stories widely throughout society. News writing can be equated with traditional historical writings, and just as our concepts of history have been questioned and criticized, so has the news.[3] The news is the history of today. As with historical writing, news writing is an attempt to structure untidy events, with their complexities and contradictions, into an orderly, linear whole. The result is an oversimplification of reality.

It is important to understand who the media represents. Is the media's purpose to inform society about facts and events within a larger context, or is it to be an instrument of the state used to define public awareness and constrain public action? Certain facts support the latter position. The media usually supports state-held positions in the portrayal and coverage of crime stories—in part because the primary sources are members of that structure. Sources are more significant in crime stories because crime is random.[4] The information which aids in the construction of crime stories is collected primarily from government sources including the police, the courts, and official statistics. Two specific factors which restrict sources to government officials are the constant urgency to access information, coupled with journalists' professional requirements for neutrality and objectivity. Due to the pressures of daily publication, the print media often uses official information because it is easier. Objectivity is assumed to be fulfilled by those institutions because of their reputations for expertise in specialized information. By using official sources the news media presents the accepted versions of specific events, those which coincide, and are consistent with, officially accepted views of the state. The media create a specific image of society which represents the interests of the powerful as the interests of the general public. This leads to public adoption of attitudes and beliefs which coincide with, and are of benefit to, those of the state.[5]

Institutions that excercise social control, such as the police and the courts, justify courses of action based on the assumption that all members of society share common goals and definitions of acceptable behaviour which have been communally defined. These communal values are actually imposed and defined in codified laws which outline unacceptable behaviours. A false consensus which compliments the law enables social control institutions to ensure that a state of normalcy and conformity is maintained.[6] Most people's understanding of the legal structure and police establishment is via the news; the lessons provided are a particular version and vision of the social order. The news media provides a powerful vehicle through which government can disseminate its definitions of knowledge and advocate its own messages.[7] The relationship between the news media and government helps provide validity, soundness, and legitimacy to both institutions: each relies on the other for validation of its respective authority. The requirements for objectivity and impartiality in the news media causes these qualities to be projected to the justice system every time the media makes reference to the law. By doing so the media provides a vehicle for the legal system to demonstrate this attribute and maintain legitimacy. Furthermore, because the legal system's version, along with its connected social control institutions, is often emphasized by the news media, the media is used by the state as an agency of surveillance and control.[8] The relationship between crime and the media is best understood as a mutually beneficial one which dictates and legitimizes the authoritarian structure of society and aids in its survival. It is evident that a preferred edited version of an event or situation is disseminated by the media. In addition, since an event is defined by reference to a state created status quo, it remains removed from the experience of ordinary citizens. As a result, media created news ignores social differences and complies with the interests of the state by concealing the process of news development in the name of authenticity, continuity and consistency.

The news media contributes to a process of state indoctrination based on public consent to accommodate state institutions. State institutions, while purporting to be well intentioned and consensually based, function for special interest groups of the wealthy and powerful. As a result, the media can seldom present a responsible debate, but must accommodate these special interests. Unlike totalitarian societies, democratic societies manufacture consent in a manipulative manner, which Noam Chomsky defines as "brainwashing under freedom."[9]

The press and the intellects are held to be fiercely independent, hypercritical, antagonistic to the 'establishment', in an adversary relation to the state.... The more vigorous the debate, the better the system of propaganda is served, since the tacit unspoken assumptions are more forcefully implanted.[10]

When disseminating the news, the media's primary responsibility is to transmit information which coincides with the dominant social control ideology, while reinforcing the public's consensual morality. Its function is to report crime stories which confirm society's values and to define the limits of tolerance.[11] In theory the media presents itself as an impartial mechanism designed to serve the interests of the larger society through the dissemination of information. In practice it contributes to propagating the adoption of state created rules which clearly separate the saints from the sinners. The news media must be considered as an advocate for formal institutions which work to maintain the status quo.

Creating a Crime Wave

The news media influences public opinion on issues of crime and its threat to society. A crime wave is a portrayal of crime based on a theme which serves to instill fear and then legitimize increased police surveillance of particular segments of society.[12] The media, through thematic coverage of crime stories, presents a particular picture of crime and who is committing it. Most crime waves produce images of serious crimes which limit the definition of crime strictly to parameters of street crimes as opposed to crimes of domestic violence or white collar crime. By selecting news on the basis of themes, incidents are stripped away from their context and redefined within a broader generalized category. For example, a crime wave occurred in New York in late 1976 with a reported surge of violence against the elderly. Along with the moral panic came ideal victims, the elderly, and typical offenders, black and hispanic youths. The news media ran articles for seven weeks. Although the image presented was of violence towards the elderly, statistics from the New York Police Department did not confirm the alleged crime wave. Although 28 percent of the media coverage reported gruesome murders, there was a 19 percent decrease in homicides of the elderly as compared to the previous year.[13] The media can manipulate facts to present a skewed reality.

The process of news gathering must be viewed in light of its dependent relationship with social control institutions. Media organizations rely exclusively on the police to provide summaries of crime incidents, so the police have the power to promote or to destroy the media's constructions. These constructed crime waves emerge in the media and policing officials use their news making powers to control their size, depending on what their agenda requires. Although news reporting plays an important role in formulating public opinion and directing future action, it may also be used to validate past behaviour and actions. Articles might be written to reaffirm, maintain, or reproduce popular myths about crime.[14]

Although crime waves generally exist only with the collaboration of several media sources, the following highlights a crime wave which was created on a smaller scale in order to justify negative treatment towards blacks by Toronto police. In July 1992 a series of three articles entitled "The Jamaican Connection" by Timothy Appleby appeared in the *Globe & Mail*. They reported on the apparent upsurge of crime by Jamaicans in Canada, particularly Toronto. The articles focused on young Jamaicans needing restraint because of their increased criminality. It also helped blur allegations of police racism being made against the Toronto Metropolitan Police Force.

The first article in the series, "Island Crime Wave Spills Over," centred around the belief that, because of the wave of Jamaican immigration into Canada and that Jamaica's crime rate is one of the highest in the world, the black crime rate has increased in Canada. In the article, West Kingston, Jamaica was described as, "...the toughest slums in the Caribbean [which] pulsates with life and the threat of death. Reggae music thunders from giant banks of loudspeakers. Rowdy bar patrons spill into graffiti-scarred alleyways where small bonfires burn. Marijuana smoke of mind-addling potency hangs in the air." The island's poverty and political polarization were outlined as the primary causes for Jamaica having one of the highest crime rates in the world. The journalist used police-gathered, ethnically-based crime data which targeted young Jamaican males as the group most responsible for committing crimes in Toronto "in an explosion of guns and crack cocaine." The journalist relied on quotes from the police to support his statements.

The article contradicted its basic premise by stating that those black youths who committed crimes were born in Canada and not Jamaica. Suggestions were made that gangs from Jamaica are affiliated with Canadians of Jamaican descent to explain the apparent contradiction. Although officials from Jamaica denied this link between their residents and those in Toronto, the article attempted to prove one by pointing to the fact that Canadians of Jamaicans descent have and retain a Jamaican accent. The article stated that since the Jamaican police do not have a computer system tourist visas are granted without a criminal record check, allowing easy access into Jamaica for Canadians of Jamaican descent involved in crime. Apart from the increase in Jamaican immigration, visas, and visits, the lack of a traditional nuclear family structure in Jamaica was described as contributing to increased criminality in Canada. The wave of immigration in the 1950s, 1970s, and 1980s, as well as the development of partisan political tribalism in Jamaica with the People's National Party and the opposition Jamaican Labour Party, all contributed to the breakdown of the family structure. A final justification for the increased criminality of Jamaicans was slavery, which instilled a rebellious, aggressive quality in the people.

In the second article, "The Twisted Arm of the Law", a link was made between Jamaica's brutal police force and the reaction of Canadians of Jamaican descent to Toronto police. The article alleged that the distrust expressed by Jamaican- Canadians towards the Metro Toronto police was related to an instinctive unease felt towards the Jamaican police force which is alleged to be heavy-handed; in 1991 they killed 205 people. The example was the killing of Raymond Lawrence, who was shot by Toronto police after having allegedly threatened a police officer with a knife. Lawrence had entered Canada illegally from Jamaica nine months before his death. The article stated that the Jamaican police kill approximately 200 people every year "usually with high-powered rifles in what are almost invariably described as shootouts." The situation is quite different if one is shot during a shootout where both sides are equally armed, as opposed to being shot when armed with a knife. This argument was an attempt by the *Globe & Mail* to explain the upsurge in police killings of blacks in Toronto by imputing that young Jamaicans, due to their pre-existing fears, incited an extreme police response. The first article of the series had stated that most of the youths involved in crime were Canadian-born, and would therefore have had no experience with the Jamaican police force and would not have these pre-established biases towards police. This discrepancy was addressed by claiming that perceptions about authority are passed along the generations, and by reading overseas papers.

The remainder of the article detailed numerous accounts of corruption and abuse by the Jamaican police force. As well, the lack of criminal accountability for its officers was discussed in a manner which falsely implied that Canadian officers are held criminally responsible for their actions. It was pointed out that the lack of computers and surveillance equipment might be a reason for the corruption. In the final paragraphs of the article, Arnold Auguste, publisher of the Toronto based black-readership newspaper *Share*, refuted the argument: "My sense is that when black people see a police officer, they don't pull a gun, they run like hell." Auguste's statement was used to create the impression that the article provided a balanced account by presenting an opposing perspective, but the comment was neither placed in the context of the article, nor was it substantiated.

In the final article of the series, "Identifying the Problem," an attempt was made to connect Canadians of Jamaican origin and other black Canadians. The article implicated Canadians of Jamaican origin as the principal perpetrators of crime in Toronto, and imputed clear distinctions within the black community. It was an attempt to divide and conquer, and to discourage solidarity among the members of the black community by separating people according to national origins. However, when a Canadian of Jamaican origin is apprehended by police, he is considered to be a black youth irrespective of his roots. Police usually acknowledge that they cannot distinguish specific ethnicities. While Canadians of Jamaican origin may hold a distinct view of crime and the police, in the police view all blacks are the same.

Black community leaders affirm that there are legitimate concerns about how Metro Toronto police officers treat members of the black community as a whole. The highly competitive white-dominated environ-ment, as well as major concerns about police racism, are potential catalysts for friction between police and the black community. As a result, young people feel alienated because they are treated as foreigners in their own land. The education system, which separates students according to perceived ability, is also acknowledged as a contributing factor to the high drop-out rate among young blacks. These comments were disregarded in the news article, and quotes from non-Jamaican blacks were included,

> "When you talk about Jamaicans, what comes to mind is the Mafia and the Italians a very small percentage that tainted the whole community.... Of course there is Jamaican crime. I'm not going to stick my head in the sand, and there's more Jamaican crime than, say, from Trinidad or Barbados."

Once again, as in the first article of the series, the waves of immigration in the 1970s and 1980s were targeted, along with the lack of two-parent homes, as the primary reasons for increased Jamaican criminality. A Canadian Metro Toronto police officer of Jamaican origin who was quoted in the article placed fault with the Canadian government about the manner in which it had initially permitted black immigration. The government had first allowed female domestics to enter, so many women were separated from their children, who remained in Jamaica. This ignores the fact that the majority of young Jamaican-Canadians living in Toronto were born in Canada.

The remainder of the article reaffirmed, using police-based accounts, that Jamaican-Canadians do commit most of Toronto's street crimes. Police sources cited in the article were described glowingly as, "a New York based posse investigator regarded as the top U.S. authority on the topic." The article also used statistics compiled by a black prisoners' advocacy group which concluded that forty percent of the prisoners in several Toronto-area jails were black, even though blacks comprise only six to eight percent of the population. These figures did not reveal how many prisoners were Jamaican-Canadian. The article did not question the discrepancy in light of police racism and systemic institutionalized discrimination; rather the statistics were used as an indicator that Jamaicans-Canadians do commit most crimes. Claims were loosely substantiated, with the figures being coupled to information about arrest rates. As a supplement, several blacks from Guyana, Barbados and Trinidad expressed similar attitudes.

The *Toronto Sun* also featured articles in May and June 1992 which accused the Ontario government of provoking a confrontation with the Metro police force by reviving a race relations task force to investigate police misconduct. They alluded to the police officers' distrust of the task force and the "incendiary comments that the police were shooting unarmed black children."[15] The newspaper also voiced displeasure over the appointment of Dudley Laws, president of the Black Action Defence Committee, to the panel reviewing police use of force. The *Toronto Sun* also labelled young Jamaicans as "the sole custodians of Black crime" in Toronto.[16]

On August 4, 1992 journalist Ewart Walters wrote two opposing articles in the *Spectrum*, an alternative newspaper for the black community, refuting the *Globe & Mail*'s allegations and accusing the newspaper of unprofessional journalism. In the first article, "Vicious Backlash," he accused the *Globe* of being part of a right-wing attack on Jamaican communities in Canada. He stated that it was a backlash in response to a report on racism the black community had initiated which confirmed allegations that racism is pervasive in Ontario. The *Globe & Mail* series was an attempt to implicate Jamaicans, specifically to divide the black community. In addition, the article's assertions coincided with claims previously made by Toronto's police union. The union had repeatedly excused the shootings of unarmed black men in Toronto by emphasizing the apparent increased crime rate among these blacks. They proposed, as a solution, the compilation of race-based crime statistics. The *Spectrum* stated "a campaign has been directed at the Government of Ontario to weaken its resolve to fight racism and curb police excesses on the grounds that it is not police excesses, but monstrous Black crime."

In Walters' second *Spectrum* article, "Tell the Children the Truth," an historical analysis was presented to counter the *Globe & Mail*'s claims. The conclusion was that "much of this bout of sensationalism against Jamaicans is opinion, innuendo, speculation, gossip, untruth, hearsay and plain, outright lies." Walters stated that the *Globe*'s assertion that marriage is rare in Jamaica was false. According to statistics compiled by the Statistics Institute of Jamaica, of 2.3 million Jamaicans there were 13,254 marriages in 1991 constituting .53 marriages per capita. Statistics Canada revealed that in 1991, of 27.3 million Canadians there were 188,660 marriages constituting .69 marriages per capita. There was not a significant difference in marriage rates in 1991, when 1.06 percent of Jamaicans compared to 1.38 percent of Canadians married.

The *Globe & Mail* articles also attacked parenting by Jamaican women, blaming them for bringing their teenage sons to Canada and allowing them to become criminals. The *Spectrum* article refuted this, reporting that the wave of female immigration occurred in the 1950s and 1960s, not in the 1970s and 1980s, so the sons of these women would now be in their forties and not the young Jamaicans allegedly committing crimes. The *Globe* confined its use of statistics to arrest rates as opposed to criminal records of conviction rates to support its arguments. All that was proved was that the black community is over policed and blacks are more likely to be targeted and arrested by police. This use of arrest records in isolation was inconclusive and intentionally manipulative. The use of conviction rates could not adequately support the argument that Jamaicans caused most of the street crimes in Toronto since it cannot be assumed that the court system does not hold the same attitudes as the police about the Jamaican community.

Walters' article stated that the *Globe & Mail*, which had rarely published articles on Jamaicans, had in one month attempted to make up for lost time. The *Globe* series denied Jamaican history and culture and did not mention the social, educational and employment circumstances faced by Jamaicans in Canada. Furthermore, the article did not refer to people born in Canada as Canadian, implying that blacks born here are not true Canadians. The *Spectrum* articles accused the *Globe & Mail* of elitism choosing descriptions such as "bleak" and "battered" for a Jamaican police inspector's office and police vehicles.

The significance of the series must be viewed in the context of the existing social climate. An analysis of media- created moral panics must acknowledge the implications of the media story rather than the incident itself. By creating a panic about Jamaican crime, accusations of police brutality could be invalidated. The black communities of Toronto and Montreal were voicing their concerns regarding the ill-treatment and harassment by police towards members of their communities. The primary allegation was of racism by police officers. The *Globe & Mail*'s coverage, in a series which implicated Jamaican-Canadians as being justifiably feared and requiring increased policing, legitimized the unjustified police violence, including the killing of blacks—not all of whom were Jamaican-Canadian. The gate was opened to increased police surveillance. As a result of the impact of the articles, a Catch-22 situation developed within the black community. By specifically targeting Jamaican-Canadians as the primary crime perpetrators, the series exacerbated divisions in the black community based on national origin. The black community's position as a unified group was weakened by the allegations of black-based criminal activity, especially when they voiced their concerns about police brutality. The police attitude of 'all blacks look alike' negatively impacted on the whole community, whose members were all, potentially, subject to questionable and excessive treatment by police.

Analysis — Montreal *Gazette*, June 1995

An analysis of coverage of the police in the Montreal *Gazette* for June 1995 was conducted to assess this news service's portrayal of the police. That month had extensive coverage of policing because of questionable action by Montreal Urban Community Police and the Quebec Provincial Police (Sûreté du Québec). Montreal's *Gazette*, as well as Montreal's two alternative newspapers the *Mirror* and *Hour*, were analyzed. During June the *Gazette* published 77 articles on the police, the *Mirror* published four articles, and *Hour* published eight articles.

Three main police related controversies were extensively covered throughout June in the *Gazette*. They were: the trial of five officers charged in the beating of Richard Barnabé; the fatal shooting of Martin Suazo; and the questionable tactics of the Sûreté du Québec (SQ). The entertainment weeklies, *Mirror* and *Hour,* restricted their coverage to the shooting of Martin Suazo. Background information relating to the controversies is important for an understanding of media positions. The alleged facts presented were claims made by the media and cannot be unreservedly accepted as actual fact.

The Richard Barnabé Trial

On the evening of December 14, 1993 the MUC police received a call from a woman at her home reporting that she heard the sound of shattering glass and a man yelling. Two MUC officers responded to the call. The man, Richard Barnabé, who had broken a church window, jumped into his car and drove away when the police arrived. The two officers, as well as numerous others who joined in the chase, pursued Barnabé to the driveway of his brother's house in Laval. By this time there were 12 to 15 officers on the scene. The officers alleged that he was yelling and out-of-control, that a number of police were needed to restrain him, pin him to the ground and handcuff him. Barnabé suffered abrasions on his elbows, knees and head from being dragged along the driveway. Blood stains were found on the driveway and the hood of the police car, and a clump of bloody hair was hanging from the ceiling of the car which transported him to Station 44. Although clearly injured, the officers took him to the station rather than to a hospital. Once in the holding cell the officers alleged that Barnabé was uncooperative and irrational when they attempted to strip-search him.

It is not known who called the ambulance, but when it arrived, Barnabé was lying unconscious in a pool of urine on his stomach with his hands handcuffed behind his back. He had suffered a broken nose, broken and torn sinus cartilage, broken ribs which had snapped off at the spine, loosened teeth with one tooth lodged in the back of his throat, black eyes, as well as extensive face, elbow and knee abrasions which were the result of being dragged across asphalt. The officers involved had nearly beaten him to death. The attending physician concluded that Barnabé's breathing had been impaired due to blood dripping into his respiratory system, coupled with the fact that he had been lying on his stomach with his hands cuffed behind his back. His impaired breathing caused cardiac arrest which lasted twenty minutes. This caused his brain to liquify and, as a result, he suffered irreversible brain damage and never regained consciousness. He remained unconscious for 29 months and died on May 2, 1996.

It was later discovered that Barnabé had broken the church window to talk to the parish priest about conflicts with his ex-girlfriend, who had denied him visitation rights with their son during the approaching Christmas holidays. Five officers, Pierre Bergeron, André Lapointe, Louis Samson,

Michel Vadenboncoeur and Manon Cadotte, were criminally charged with aggravated assault and assault causing bodily harm in the beating of Richard Barnabé. Because he survived for over a year the officers could not be charged with murder or manslaughter. The Criminal Code of Canada states that additional charges stemming from a particular incident must be laid within one year of the original charges.

There were a total of 29 articles in the *Gazette*'s coverage of the Richard Barnabé trial, (See Appendix 1) most written by Lisa Fitterman. Throughout the trial there was contradictory evidence regarding what actually happened between Barnabé and the officers in the cell. Although the excessive beating was not warranted, Barnabé was unarmed and handcuffed, the charged officers attempted to justify their actions by describing him as aggressive and uncooperative. Despite contradictory evidence, in the June 5th coverage Fitterman wrote that the question to be addressed was whether the officers had "used excessive force to restrain Barnabé, who had strenuously objected to being undressed and searched in the cell." The claim that he was violent and erratic while in the cell was an unsubstantiated one made by the officers involved. Nonetheless, Fitterman asserted that Barnabé had made violent objections. Some members of the mainstream media appear to be willing to accept the official police version of events as fact, without consideration of opposing points of view.

In the June 12 coverage Fitterman addressed the contradictory trial evidence by stating "Was he a weak man, with little muscle, who pined for his son? Or was he strong, aggressive and delusional, shouting about the mafia, the devil, God and pins and needles pricking him?" Regardless of whether or not Barnabé was aggressive, he did not deserve to be beaten almost to death by several officers. Trained officers should be familiar with restraint techniques which do not result in the extensive injuries Barnabé suffered. The *Gazette* coverage focused on an attempt to determine whether or not Barnabé had been aggressive. The aggressive behaviour by the officers involved was not mentioned. Other unaddressed questions include: at what point in the beating would Barnabé have been physically able to aggressively resist, given the extent of his injuries? And, more importantly, how could six officers feel threatened by this unarmed, injured, and handcuffed man in a holding cell of a police station?

In the June 17 coverage, in a paragraph following a detailed description of Barnabé's extensive injuries, the article stated that most of the evidence against the police officers was circumstantial. The *Gazette* article reiterated the prosecutor's point that "there were a crucial 15 minutes during which nobody except Barnabé and the officers themselves knew what was going on in the cell." It then restated the officers' claims that Barnabé was violent. On June 27 an article again stated: "The Crown's evidence, although graphic and dramatic, was circumstantial, although there was damning testimony coming from Urgence Santé ambulance attendant Robert Belanger, who overheard a superior officer telling the constables not to beat, "tabasser," Barnabé too badly." The ambulance attendant's testimony confirmed that the Crown's case was not purely circumstantial. The comment suggested malicious intent, since a superior officer acknowledged that Barnabé was being beaten but he was only concerned that they not go too far. The constant repetition that the prosecution's evidence was circumstantial weakened the Crown's case in the eyes of the public, who incorrectly assume that circumstantial evidence is always less reliable than direct evidence.

In the day by day account of the court proceeding, the *Gazette* articles expressed sympathy for the accused officers throughout the trial. In the June 3 coverage, Fitterman described Manon Cadotte crying while giving her testimony. In the June 6 coverage she concluded the article with Vadenboncoeur's account that "he was in shock, that he never thought something like this could happen." In the June 26 coverage Fitterman quoted Barnabé's sister, "This is tough, but I'll tell you, it's probably tougher for the officers." Fitterman then outlined the stressed condition of the accused officers. She said, "She is probably right. The officers' faces are drawn and their bodies tense. They walk with their eyes fixed straight ahead. Bergeron, the senior officer charged in the case, has lost about ten pounds." This expression of sympathy was exclusively for the accused police officers; the same officers who collaborated in beating Richard Barnabé until his brain was liquified, and who ultimately caused his death. In other trials involving civilians media accounts do not usually express such concern for the accused.

On June 26, 1995 four of the five officers accused were found guilty of assault causing bodily harm; Manon Cadotte was found not guilty. On June 27 the *Gazette* covered the verdict with six articles. Once again Fitterman presented a sympathetic portrayal of the now convicted officers. In the front page article, "4 Cops Found Guilty; Stunned Officers Cry After Verdict; One is Innocent", she stated that the officers "shook their heads and sobbed in disbelief." She also wrote that the four officers appeared stunned by the verdict.

> In the prisoner's box, Lapointe was muttering, "This can't be. This can't be." Vadenboncoeur had collapsed, crying, his elbows on his lap. Samson absentmindedly rubbed his back to comfort him.... Bergeron had his left arm wrapped protectively around his wife, who had minutes earlier comforted him as he cried in the courtroom. He walked as if he was sleepwalking and not seeing anything.

Fitterman once again stated that Bergeron had lost ten pounds during the trial. She also elaborated on the strain for the Barnabé family. In the concluding paragraph of the article Fitterman placed partial blame on Richard's brother, Raymond Barnabé, who is an MUC officer. On the night of the beating Richard Barnabé had driven to his brother's house in Laval. Although aware of the officers in his driveway, Raymond Barnabé did not attempt to find out what was going on. Fitterman concluded the article on the following note, "What if Raymond Barnabé had gone outside to ask what was going on when his wife informed him there were lots of police officers and a man lying on the ground? What if he hadn't simply turned on the lights to help his colleagues do their job more efficiently?" This was an attempt to alleviate the responsibility of the indicted officers by shifting partial blame to Raymond Barnabé. It suggests that, had he gone outside to discover his brother on the ground, he could have prevented the incident. This implies that Raymond Barnabé would not have stopped a beating of an individual if it had not been his brother. This exemplifies the attitude that the public should not concern itself with police acts of violence against people unless they are personally involved; that it would have been acceptable for

Raymond Barnabé to turn on a light for the police to carry out their duties if the victim had been a stranger, but it was unfortunate that he did not take action when it was his brother who was being beaten.

In the second front-page article "Don't Lose Faith in Us: Police Chief", MUC police chief Jacques Duchesneau outlined possible surveillance strategies, including the installation of 24-hour video cameras in holding cells to avoid a similar incident. What was the rationale? The implication is that if officers were aware that they were being taped, they might engage in less brutal conduct.

In the same article a defense witness, referred to as "Manitoba's chief medical examiner", testified at the trial that Barnabé was suffering from a medical syndrome called excited delirium, which had caused his heart to stop. He stated that persons suffering from this condition often die in police custody, and placing them lying face down increases the risk. He acknowledged that all previously documented cases of excited delirium involved the use of alcohol or drugs while Barnabé had used neither. The prosecution witness, Dr. Mark Angle, testified that Barnabé's coma resulted from oxygen deprivation to the brain which was caused by impaired breathing resulting from a broken nose and sinus cartilage, blood dripping into his respiratory system, three broken ribs which were snapped off at the spine and a broken tooth lodged in his throat. The chief continued to maintain that Barnabé's heart stopped because he was lying on his stomach. Following the report of the chief's statement, the *Gazette* referred to the defence expert's testimony which claimed that Barnabé had been suffering from excited delirium. Although the jury had concluded that the four officers were guilty; Fitterman continued to allude to the defence argument that the officers were not responsible for Barnabé's comatose condition and deny their direct responsibility for his injuries.

On June 28 a front page *Gazette* article again discussed the Richard Barnabé verdict. Its tone reinforced the belief that the guilty verdict, in and of itself, sent a message to the police—whether or not the officers served a prison term. Various criminology academics were asked to comment on the conviction. Criminologist André Normandeau supported the *Gazette*'s view, "The message to police is, 'You have to really have a professional spirit and not use extreme force.... Seeing cops convicted in criminal court has a heavy symbolic weight, much more that a guilty verdict from the police-ethics commission." Normandeau stated that attitudes concerning violence had been evolving within the police force since the 1987 fatal shooting of Anthony Griffin, but provided no supporting information. Since Griffin's death there have been numerous questionable deaths at the hands of the MUC police. Another criminologist stated that he believed the verdict would force officers to be more prudent with suspects behind closed doors. The article continued with an opposing view by criminologist Jean-Paul Brodeur, who affirmed that he had not seen an improvement regarding excessive force within the MUC police. He pointed to the recent killings of Paolo Romanelli, Martin Suazo and Phillipe Ferraro to support his belief. The article also quoted MUC police chief Duchesneau, who stated that the convicted officers would not necessarily lose their jobs. Although individuals with a criminal record cannot join the police force, serving officers who are convicted of a criminal offence may retain their employment. That a police chief would consider retaining convicted officers is baffling.

In a front page article, "Chief Urged to Fire Cops in Barnabé Case," civil rights groups, angered by the MUC police chief's suggestion that the four officers be reintegrated into the force, urged chief Duchesneau to fire the officers. Dan Philip, president of the Black Coalition of Quebec, said, "Can you imagine these guys putting on their uniforms again, arresting people and keeping prisoners in custody? You would be reintegrating criminals into the police force. All they would have received was a slap on the wrist for what they did. The public will not stand for it." The article was followed by another article, "Many Quebec Policemen Have Faced Serious Charges," which listed 11 cases since 1984 in which officers were charged with various offenses. In all but one of the incidents the officers were exonerated and had remained on active duty, were promoted, or took early retirement. The exception was an officer who received a life sentence for the April 1986 murder of two police officers during an investigation of a robbery by Sgt. Serge Lefebvre in Ste. Foy.

On July 13 Judge Benjamin Greenberg handed down his sentences for the four indicted officers. Pierre Bergeron and Louis Samson received 90 days or 45 weekends in jail and a one year probation. André Lapointe was given 60 days or 30 weekends in jail and a one year probation. Michel Vadenboncoeur received 180 hours of community service and two years probation, with the community service to be performed at a centre for young offenders or a long-term care hospital excluding Nôtre-Dame-de-la-Merci, where Barnabé was hospitalized. Hours after receiving the sentences the officers filed appeals. Judge Greenberg explained the leniency of his sentences, stating that his role was 'not to reflect the popular view but to administer justice pure and simple.' He maintained that the officers were not criminals in need of rehabilitation because they posed no threat to society and that there was no evidence indicating they had intended to hurt Barnabé or had acted with malice. But the question remains, how did he end up in a coma which lasted 29 months until he died? Greenberg also said that the officers had already suffered tremendously; been stigmatized by the media, ostracized by the public and faced the prospect of losing their jobs. He did not repeal their right to carry a firearm, which is the usual procedure when someone is convicted of a criminal offence, because he stated that it would cost them their jobs. This is false. In the aftermath of the 1987 killing of Anthony Griffin in Montreal the officer's right to carry a firearm was revoked and, rather than costing him his job, he was transferred and promoted to the wiretapping section of the MUC.

A crucial factor in the sentencing was the possibility of the officers being fired. The judge believed that this would be sufficient punishment. Loss of employment is not a consideration in sentencing for others; when someone is convicted and sentenced for a criminal offence to a prison term, they will probably lose their job. There was also no certainty that the convicted officers would be fired. Before the sentences were handed down the chief had already stated that it was possible that the officers would remain on the force.

The day after the sentencing the police brotherhood held a news conference during which union president Yves Prud'homme urged the chief not to fire the officers. He admitted that the officers had made errors in judgment, but believed that their lives and careers should not be torn apart. He blamed the controversy over the Barnabé affair on the media, budget cuts, and MUC police management, which had been negligent in informing its staff of the dangers involved in restraining prisoners on their stomachs. He criticized the 'half truths and rumours and sensational headlines during the trial when people are supposed to be presumed innocent until proven guilty.' This comment about negative media coverage is unjustified in light of the *Gazette*'s sympathetic reporting about the officers. On July 15 the police brotherhood placed a full page ad in *La Presse* to ask "why we (the police) are living in insecurity," and responding: "when we don't use weapons, but through error or accident we might cause injuries, must we be amputated?"

Chief Duschesneau held a news conference July 17, 1995, where he stated that he believed that the officers involved had committed only two errors. They were: 1) they did not take Barnabé to the hospital from Laval even though he was clearly hurt, and 2) the officers tried to take his clothes off in the cell. The chief announced that he would wait for the appeals of the conviction and outcome of the police ethics committee hearing before deciding about the officers' future employment. Until then the officers were suspended without pay, but their salaries would be paid by the police brotherhood.

In December 1997, in the aftermath of the Barnabé incident, the Quebec Police Ethics Commission suspended two of the officers, André Lapointe and Michel Vadeboncoeur, for 140 days and 120 days respectively, for their role in the beating. The chief allowed a deal to be struck so that the officers could trade in their vacation time, a total of 90 days, to return to work earlier. Chief Duschesneau stated, "Is it fair to their families that they be out of jobs and out of a salary for so long?"[17] This move caused friction between the commission and the former police chief. Public Security Minister Pierre Bélanger urged the MUC to stand by the commission's decision, however, interim chief Claude Rochon did not back down, believing that the decision was legal. Serge Fortin, a spokesman for the police ethics commission, stated that although the MUC went directly against their decision, the commission does not have the power to enforce them to carry out the sanctions. The two remaining convicted officers were dismissed from the force.

The Fatal Shooting of Martin Suazo

On May 31, 1995 a 37-year-old MUC officer fatally shot Martin Suazo, a 23-year-old Peruvian man, in the back of the neck as he lay on the ground waiting to be handcuffed. Suazo and two others had just shoplifted five pairs of jeans from a Montreal store. The store owner hailed a police car, and told the officers that he had just been robbed and that the suspects had fled by car. The officers then radioed to police headquarters and requested a roadblock. Once apprehended Suazo and the others were ordered out of their car and told to lie down on the pavement. The officers had their guns drawn throughout, even though Suazo and the others were unarmed.

When the ambulance arrived attendants found Suazo lying on the pavement unattended while a group of police officers stood across the road. No ambulance had been called but one arrived because it was parked nearby and the driver decided to follow the police car with flashing lights. No police officers were in the hospital-bound ambulance. Twenty-five minutes later, the police arrived at the hospital.

The officer involved in the shooting was placed on sick leave with pay. His name was not revealed to the public or the Suazo family until several months later when the Crown decided not to lay criminal charges. The two other individuals involved were arrested and charged with robbery, conspiracy and possession of stolen goods.

There were 12 articles covering the fatal shooting of Martin Suazo in the *Gazette*. (See Appendix 1) The majority of the articles described the shoplifting incident as a robbery. Implicit in the use of the term robbery is the assumption that a hold-up occurred; which created an impression of violence and inflated the severity of the original shoplifting charge.

Although Martin Suazo was shot on May 31 and died in hospital on June 1, the *Gazette* did not report the story until June 2 on page three. The article reported that the police shot Suazo while he was lying on the ground waiting to be handcuffed. The *Gazette* called the shoplifting "a grab-and-run theft" and described the store owner as having a bleeding face and a torn shirt when he hailed a police car. The owner had chased the three and was allegedly punched by one of the individuals as he tried to wrestle the bag of jeans from the woman. The final paragraphs of the article concentrated on the MUC's re-arming of their officers in 1991. Their weapons had been changed from single-action revolvers to double-action revolvers which are less likely to fire accidentally. The implication was that the incident might not have been an accident.

On June 3 a page three *Gazette* article about the Suazo shooting described him as co-operating with the police when he was shot. An eye-witness stated, "[h]e had his hands up in front of him and was in a crouching position, about to lie down on the road when the officer shot him....You would have thought they were mass murderers, the way the he (officer) was screaming. To me, it seemed like the cop was overreacting." The *Gazette* described the shoplifters as bandits who beat the store manager before fleeing. The article did not mention that the owner had attempted to grab the bag of jeans from the woman. Without this piece of information, and coupled with the use of the term bandits, the implication was that the shoplifters had stormed into the store, stolen the jeans, and assaulted the manager for no reason before fleeing. The Sûreté du Québec which investigated the incident, stated that the officer's gun had accidentally discharged while he was subduing Suazo prior to the completion of the investigation. The *Gazette*'s account was sympathetic to the implicated officer, reporting that he "panicked after the shooting and started screaming." The article concluded with a statement about the re-arming of the MUC force. There was no link made to a previous SQ statement that the revolver fired accidentally.

On June 4 the front page of the *Gazette* contained a picture of Martin Suazo's girlfriend, Olga Gomez, comforting his mother, Lily Salinas, with a story following on page A three. Lily Salinas, who came to Montreal from Peru because of the death of her son, stated that her son's shooting was not an accident because double-action revolvers rarely discharge without pressure being applied on the trigger. She alleged that the shooting was racially motivated. The incident was once again described as a theft rather than a shoplifting.

A June 8 article reported that the coroner had not decided whether a coroner's inquest would be called to investigate the shooting. The shoplifting incident was again described as a robbery by a grab-and-run gang. The June 9 article outlined the Quebec Human Rights Commissioner's demand for a public inquiry because of its distrust of the Sûreté du Québec investigation— which had pre-maturely concluded that the revolver had fired accidentally. The shoplifting incident was described as a robbery at a jeans store. On June 11 the *Gazette* reported a fund-raising event held by the Latin-American community to help the Suazo family raise the $1,500 needed to return Suazo's body to Peru for burial. A family friend stated that the community was angry because the police, especially the chief, had not expressed condolences to the Suazo family. The incident was described as: "The car he and two others were riding in had been stopped by police after a robbery."

There were two front-page articles in the June 17 *Gazette*, "Killings By Cops to Be Probed" and "Anger and Confusion Hit Latin American Community," accompanied by a picture of Suazo's mother, Lily Salinas. The first article stated that a public inquiry would be held into the shootings of Paolo Romanelli, who was killed by police on March 3, and Martin Suazo. The *Gazette* once again referred to the shoplifting incident as a robbery. The second article focused on the Latin American community's anger and distrust of the MUC police as well as the community's lack of political power which had hampered an early response to the shooting. It included Martin Suazo's history— his difficult life alone in a foreign land, his inability to hold a job, and his father's imprisonment. Various Latin American community representatives discussed the difficulties which their young people experience in Canada. The *Gazette* stated, "[s]ome youths feel excluded from Quebec society. Lacking social services, they try to find comfort among themselves by joining street gangs." The implication was that Suazo was involved in gang activity and that his delinquency caused his death. The *Gazette* appeared to be reducing the officer's responsibility in the unjustified shooting, quoting a South-American born taxi-driver, "[a]nyone involved in crime will await his destiny. If he stole now he would end up shooting someone sooner or later. I knew his father, he was involved in drugs. I don't know why Canada didn't deport him a long time ago."

An article, "Suazo Loved Living in Canada, Mother Recalls" had a similar theme. The father's ex-girlfriend described him as a lonely boy "who eventually fell under bad influences." The *Gazette* also reported that Suazo was on welfare when he died and had resorted to shoplifting because he could not survive. Martin Suazo's life, rather than information about who shot him was emphasized. Blame was placed on the young man who stole five pairs of jeans. While Suazo's life was being publicly scrutinized the name of the officer who shot him was not revealed to the public or to the Suazo family. The police chief placed a media ban on the name of the implicated officer until the Crown decided whether or not criminal charges would be laid.

There were numerous articles which, though not exclusively reporting on the Suazo shooting, included a summary of the incident. Apart from using a harsher terminology including bandits, gang, and robbery, many summaries did not include the facts, but relied on generalizations which portrayed Martin Suazo's shoplifting very negatively. In addition, the reporting did not describe the circumstances under which Suazo was shot, while he was lying on the ground waiting to be handcuffed. In a June 5 editorial, "Police Probes Smack of Coverup", Suazo was described as a robbery suspect. In the June 8 editorial, "Oops," Suazo was described as an immigrant from Peru, and neglected to mention that he moved to Canada as a very young child. The June 14 editorial, "SQ Probe Lacks Credibility" described Suazo as a 23-year-old unarmed robbery suspect. On June 20 in a page three article, "Police Wrong to Storm House Coroner Says", Suazo's shooting took place "after he and his companions were ordered out of a car about one kilometre from a clothing store where several pairs of jeans had been stolen." In a June 22 page seven article, "Sûreté Still Sorting Out Delay Over Statement," the incident was described as, "Suazo was shot by MUC police as he was being arrested. He and two other companions had been stopped as suspects in a robbery." In a June 22 page four report, "Groups Want Closer Study on Probes By Police," Suazo's shooting occurred "as he was being arrested after a robbery at a jeans store." Once again, in a page three article on June 27, "Convictions—Another Black Eye for Force," the description of the incident was "Suazo, suspected of robbery, was killed when he was being taken into custody." The inaccurate depiction of the incident was an attempt to portray Suazo as a young delinquent who committed a robbery and who was shot while being taken into custody.

Of the eight articles which included a summary of the Suazo shooting, only Peggy Curran's June 14 article was accurate in its description of the facts. In her article, "Police Must Be Held Accountable When They Mess

Up" she wrote: "Witnesses say Martin Omar Suazo, 23, had surrendered and was lying face down on the pavement when he was shot in the neck. Like François and Barnabé, Suazo, suspected of stealing jeans from a shop, was unarmed."

The Suazo shooting coverage in the alternative weeklies, *Mirror* and *Hour*, relied primarily on eye-witness accounts and family-related concerns rather than on official police statements. There were direct accusations of brutality against the MUC police institution. In the June 8 *Mirror* coverage, "Memories of Griffin", a witness and close friend of Martin Suazo stated that the accidental shooting excuse was similar to the one used for the Anthony Griffin case. Another witness to the shooting wondered why the officer had his gun pointing at Martin when he was on the ground. He told the *Mirror*, "The guy wasn't armed so the worst he could have done was punch him."

In the June 15 coverage, "No One's Safe," the *Mirror* published a letter from a friend of Suazo's who voiced his contempt for the MUC police for labelling the incident an accident, and for not seriously reprimanding the implicated officer. His fear of members of the MUC police was clear:

> How does a double-action weapon "accidently" go off? Why is a gun pointed at someone's skull when he is already face down and unarmed on the pavement, surrounded by five or six cops? Why do these deadly "accidents" keep happening over and over again, with total impunity to the criminals responsible, the MUC police? ...I'm not signing my name. I'm too afraid of the police.

The June 29 *Mirror* editorial, "Screw the Brotherhood," named the police brotherhood as the major problem within the MUC policing institution. The editor voiced his anger and dissatisfaction with police officers who kill unjustifiably while on duty. He stated that these exclusive rights are rooted in the illusionary danger of their duties. Regarding the Martin Suazo killing, he said, "…. the Latino arrested in connection with a minor shoplifting incident who has the right to a trial and to see the evidence against him; [he's] the one who needs protection, not the gun-wielding, flak-jacketed cop who is trained to handle stressful situations." He advised the public at large to screw the brotherhood and protect themselves against MUC officers by steering clear of them.

In the June 8 *Hour* article, "Accidents Happen," the journalist asked: "Which do you prefer? 1) Montreal is a city where the police can shoot people in the head just because they feel like it and get away with it. 2) Montreal is a city where the police carry guns that could go off accidently at any time. The problem is that one of them has to be true, and that you live here." He mentioned a conversation he had had about the Martin Suazo death with an Iraqui coffee shop owner who wanted to return to the Middle East because it was safer there. "Even in Iraq these kind of things don't happen. Yes, the secret police are very dangerous, but this kind of thing never happens with the municipal police." The journalist also discussed the Sûreté du Québec's inadequate investigations of MUC officers. The article concluded with a comment about the alleged inadequacy of the double-action revolvers.

In a June 15 letter to *Hour*, "Every Human Racist," Mr. Pigeon, possibly a police officer, expressed his concerns about the community outcry following Suazo's death. He stated that he did not believe that the entire force should be blamed for the conduct of one officer. He further asserted that every human being is racist, so why would the police any different. This letter countered earlier articles written in both *Hour* and *Mirror*, yet *Hour* chose to print it and so acknowledged opposing perspectives. Beside the letter was an article, "The Top 10 MUC Police Accidents," which outlined ten controversial incidents the MUC was involved in. It countered Pigeon's assertion that the officer who shot Suazo was a bad apple.

Several facts were made public after the Suazo incident. The police chief decided that no charges would be laid and no disciplinary action would be taken against the officer. Chief Duchesneau commented, "It's too bad someone died. It's bad for the family, it's also bad for the police officer himself. Killing a person is a tragic incident in your life."[18]

At the coroner's inquest in February 1996 ambulance driver Danny Ray testified that after Suazo was shot he was left on the pavement unattended.

There was no police officers around the body when we got there. In fact, we didn't even know there was a body in the road. We though something was happening in a nearby field where several officers had assembled.[19]

Along with leaving the critically injured Suazo unattended, the police also neglected to call for medical assistance. Ambulance attendants who happened to be parked nearby noticed a police car with flashing lights and decided to follow it. Ray's testimony regarding the position of Suazo's body contradicted that of the officers.' None of the police officers were present in the ambulance which took him to the hospital.

The Sûreté du Québec's Questionable Tactics

Five Sûreté du Québec controversies dominated *Gazette* pages in June 1995.

1) Gaetan Rivest, a former SQ detective, alleged that he and a number of officers beat a suspect until he signed a murder confession. Rivest said that the three other officers involved were still on the force.

2) On September 1, 1994, the Sûreté du Québec detained all the members of the Chambly police force, along with a number of their wives, as part of an investigation into criminal-gang activities in the region. A judicial inquiry was established to investigate the legitimacy of the raid.

3) Sûreté du Québec investigators planted evidence in a drug-smuggling case that resulted in the judge ordering a stay of proceedings in the trial of seven members of the so-called West End Gang. Four incriminating maritime lading documents with an unidentifiable fax number they planted were tagged as part of the goods seized. These documents entitled the holder to the contents of a container. The gang was being tried for smuggling 26.5 tons of hashish into the Port of Montreal in May 1994.

4) A dying man, André Desbien, taped a confession about the Sûreté du Québec coercing him into perjuring himself about evidence in the 1986 triple murder trial of Yves Plamondon, which resulted in a life sentence. He stated that the police forced him to pretend that he had direct knowledge of Plamondon's guilt in the killings.

5) The SQ probes into the MUC beating of Richard Barnabé and the shootings of Paolo Romanelli and Martin Suazo were charged with lacking credibility and impartiality. In the Suazo shooting, the SQ waited three weeks before taking a formal statement from the only eye-witness— after

they had already declared that it had been an accident. In the Barnabé case the SQ failed to inform the accused officers of their rights and also did not inform them before questioning that they were suspects in the case, thus rendering the evidence inadmissible.

There were 17 *Gazette* articles covering the tactics of the Sûreté du Québec. (See Appendix 1) Most of the coverage was negative, without the liberal sympathies expressed in the MUC police related incidents. The *Gazette* appears to have attempted to divert attention away from the MUC related incidents by shining a harsher light on their SQ counterparts.

There were seven police related editorials in June. Of the seven, five discussed the SQ tactics, one the Barnabé trial and one the shooting of Paolo Romanelli. All five of the editorials about the SQ were highly critical of their behaviour.

The *Gazette's* coverage of the SQ directed attention away from controversies surrounding the MUC police, primarily the Richard Barnabé trial and the fatal shooting of Martin Suazo. Focussing negative attention on their provincial counterparts diminished the importance of the serious allegations made against the Montreal force. The editorial, "Police Probe Smacks of Coverup," on June 5, discussed the inadequate investigation the SQ conducted into the shooting of Martin Suazo and accused them of minimizing the extent of the MUC's misconduct. But, when commenting on the possibility of criminal charges being laid against the officer involved, the editor wrote, "If criminal charges are involved, as happens in rare instances such as the current Barnabé case, officers will go to trial. This is unlikely in the Suazo case, where an officer fired on the spur of the moment; malice is almost impossible to prove." The editor erroneously assumed that malice must be proved for criminal charges to be laid. He concluded the editorial with a comment about the SQ being the primary abuser of authority, "It is bad enough when officers abuse their authority by shooting people needlessly. But this generally results from split-second decisions. Worse is the carefully thought-out policy that impedes justice in such cases. That is a greater abuse of authority." This attempted to diminish the MUC's culpability in the killings of Montreal citizens by focusing on the SQ's inability to properly and impartially investigate the incidents. The four remaining editorials had similar themes: Public Security Minister Serge Menard must take action "to restore the credibility of the provincial police force," but there was no comment about the need to restore the credibility of the MUC police.

Throughout the *Gazette* coverage, the principal accusation concerned the SQ's leniency when investigating their counterparts. However, in a June 20 article, "Evidence Not Used in Barnabé Case After SQ Faulted", the SQ were accused of harsh treatment towards the MUC police. Because the SQ investigators failed to properly read the MUC officers involved in the Barnabé beating their rights, their statements were inadmissible as evidence. The article stated that "the inadmissible statements are the latest blow to the SQ in a month that has seen its credibility buffeted by one scandal after another."

Allegations against the SQ were as serious as the MUC police responsibility for the shooting deaths and beatings; but by moving the principal problem away from Montreal, the MUC actions would lose importance. Although the numerous allegations of misconduct against the SQ were serious, they did not overshadow the culpability of the MUC police.

The Fatal Shooting of Phillipe Ferraro

The June 27 *Gazette* article, in the same issue as a report about the outcome of the Barnabé trial, contained a story, "Man Dies After 1-Hour Standoff". It involved the mysterious death of a 67-year-old man, Phillipe Ferraro, after a standoff with MUC police. The police were dispatched to his Montreal home on a domestic violence call. The man had allegedly threatened to kill his sister, who then left the house and called the police. On the police arrival, the man barricaded himself in his home and refused to surrender. The SWAT team responded by firing tear-gas into the apartment. An eye witness stated that the man then opened the door holding an axe. The SWAT team responded by firing two rubber bullets, causing him to retreat into the house. The police stormed the house and found the man dead. Police officials immediately stated that the man died of a heart attack.

Although the circumstances surrounding Ferraro's death were

questionable, the front-page article was a small part of an article reporting the Barnabé verdict. Although the Barnabé verdict dominated the first pages of the newspaper, the story deserved a wider coverage.

A June 28 *Gazette* article revealed that Ferraro had been killed by the rubber bullets. The coroner stated that Ferraro had died of "internal haemorrhaging after a rubber bullet fired by police perforated his left lung and caused abrasions in the heart." The discovery that the rubber bullets, and not a heart attack, had caused his death was not front-page news. The first *Gazette* story revealed that he had been shot twice with rubber bullets, in the second story it was revealed that the SWAT team had fired at least three bullets. In the June 27 article a witness was quoted as having seen Ferraro open the door holding an axe, while in the June 28 account, Sgt. Pierre Sangollo stated that he "came out brandishing a cement pick. That's when we fired." The *Gazette* had previously reported that Sangollo had stated that Ferraro had thrown an 18-inch cement pick at the police officers. It is unclear whether he was shot while he held the pick or after he allegedly threw it at the officers.

Sangollo was incorrect when he stated that the SWAT team had used rubber bullets twenty times in eight years without causing death or grievous injury. On March 6, 1993 Yvon Asselin was shot with rubber bullets by the SWAT team and later died in the hospital. The coroner's report was inconclusive but the shots may have been the cause of death.

The only source for the information in the article was Sangollo, the police assistant director of special investigations. In the first article the *Gazette* stated that there had been an eye witness but he was not interviewed for the second story. The only civilian statement used was by Ferraro's neighbours who said that he was an odd and sick man. One neighbour elaborated, "It was always dark in there and they never wanted to have anything to do with anyone else. It was known by everyone that they had mental problems."

Directly below the Ferraro story was "Trio Bungle Downtown Diamond Heist; Police Surround Church during Search for Armed Suspects," which described the MUC police search for three armed diamond thieves in downtown Montreal. The article included a picture of three armed police officers wearing bullet proof vests discussing strategy. The story reinforced the message that police crime fighting is dangerous work and that their extreme precautions are necessary to protect the lives and property of citizens.

Creating a Balance

Public opinion can be manipulated by the exclusion or selection of information in media reports. On June 3, the day after the initial report of Suazo's fatal shooting by police, the *Gazette* front page article was "Blacks, Police Are Patching Things Up," which described the improving relations between the police and blacks in Côte-des-Neiges and included a large photograph. The previous day Suazo's death was reported in a smaller page three article with no photograph. The June 3 article asserted that there had been an enormous improvement in relations between the MUC police and the black community. The picture of two white police officers in a convenience store with a smiling black man behind the counter contained a dual message, a black store-owner comfortable with the police, and the inferrence that peace existed between the two groups. Members of the black community stated in the article that there had been an overall improvement in the attitudes and community relations by the police. The *Gazette* linked, without explanation, the 1991 Marcellus François incident and the supposedly improved relations, even though the officers involved were exonerated. There were three other sources, Noel Alexander, president of the Jamaican Association of Montreal, Peter Haywood, a black community member, and a man who asked not to be identified, who all substantiated the claim.

The *Gazette*'s initial reports on the Suazo incident implicated the police, then an article attempted to diffuse the controversy and eliminate allegations of police racism. The article implied that, although Suazo was Hispanic, his colour was not related to his killing. The implicit comparison was with the black community, which for the previous eight years had accused the police of racism, and had now regained their trust in the police. The illusion was of the *Gazette*'s neutrality in its coverage of stories involving deaths caused by police, while the second article attempted to negate any police responsibility. It was also an attempt to divide ethnic communities and to provide a balance to the negative image of the MUC policing institution. Page two also had two smaller articles, "Not All Officers Show Good Will" and "Some Don't See an Improvement," which refuted claims of improved police relations with the black community.

During the first weeks of the Suazo coverage, through other controversial police incidents, there were pro-police articles. A June 18 front page article "Foot Patrol Gives Constables Time for 'Little Trouble'," appeared with a large photograph of two foot patrol officers chatting with a homeless man. The article continued on the whole of page four with the heading: "Getting to Know the Street People: Beat Cops in Their Baseball Caps Get More Smiles Than Scowls," and described a day in the life of two MUC beat cops along with the officers' tremendous public relations and crime fighting abilities. There were five photographs:

1) Two youths being handcuffed by the two officers with the caption, "Police officers handcuff a youth on a catwalk at the York Theatre building."

2) Officer Parker talking to a smiling young East Indian, "Ste. Catherine St. merchant Shalini Tripathi talks to Parker."

3) Officer Roy entering the abandoned York theatre where graffiti stating, 'Trespassers Will Be Eaten,' is visible. The caption read, "Roy checks one of the rooms in the rundown York Theatre building."

4) The two officers helping an elderly woman cross the street. The caption was, "Beat cops Roy (left) and Parker help Doreen Legrand, who is partially blind, across Ste. Catherine St."

5) Officer Roy helping an elderly man to walk through a field. The caption read: "Far right, Constable Roy helps Gilles Vidal get to a shady spot where he can cool off."

The article mentioned the recent shooting of Martin Suazo and the trial of the officers involved in the beating of Richard Barnabé. When asked about the recent trial controversy, Roy responded: "People are talking to us about Barnabé. It's hard for us to stay impartial but we have to.... We can't dirty these guys, because they wear the same uniform." The implication was that police officers must support each other regardless of the circumstances. The journalist followed Roy's statement with "Parker and Roy get more smiles than scowls." Roy also commented that police officers who patrol in cars do not get enough credit. "They're the ones who should get the handshakes and claps on their back."

Photographs increase the visual impact of news stories and create a permanent public impression. The two articles included six photographs, and there were thirteen additional photographs involving the police in the *Gazette* in June. Of the thirteen photographs, three involved police crime fighting activities, two were of police officials and four were of the officers involved in the beating of Richard Barnabé. There were only five photographs of the victims in the incidents, Richard Barnabé, Martin Suazo and Lily Salinas. The photographs and captions in the articles projected a lasting image of on-going commendable police activities and diminished the allegations of brutality and corruption.

Both of the articles appeared in the *Gazette* during the police controversies in an attempt to create a balance. Bad press about policing activities was neutralized with good press. Although crime stories implicating the criminalized police were balanced with stories about good cops, the same does not hold true when citizens from a specific community are implicated in crimes. Criminalized communities do not have the influence to counter the deviance label with more positive perspectives.

Another example of preferential treatment was the *Gazette*'s silence about a young woman who was assaulted by the MUC drug squad after they mistook her for a drug dealer. Such an incident further reinforced the brutal image of the MUC police. *Hour*, covered the story in its June 8 issue. Venelina Ghiaurov was using the toilet in a Montreal coffee shop when she heard men yelling at her to open the door. Before she could react she was hit in the face by the bathroom door and three plainclothes officers forced her out of the bathroom and through the crowded café with her underpants still around her ankles. Once outside, one of the officers held a gun to her head. When Ghiaurov asked the officers if she could put on her underclothes she was ignored as they searched her. She continued to plead unsuccessfully with the officers. After the search was completed she was allowed to pull up her underpants. She stated that one of the officers said, "Okay, now you're finished with the panicking. So get out of here because we've got a job to do." Another officer attempted to apologize for the comment: "This is normal, you know? You've got to realize these guys are just doing their job." She went to the hospital and was diagnosed as having suffered a concussion. The incident was not reported in the *Gazette*.

When incidents of excessive and lethal police use of force occur it is police brutality. The media often implicates the individual officer involved as the wrong-doer without implicating the entire policing system. In most crime stories the individual is the focus, the situation or event is individualized, and social circumstances are denied. Such particularizing allows the media to deflect attention away from the wider social context. The complexities existing beyond the individual are ignored, as is an examination of the policing institution as a whole. The media diverts attention from the cause, the policing institution, to the symptom, the individual officer involved in the shooting. The officer involved has personal faults in a specific situation, but the structural factors and cultural framework which may have led to the illegitimate use of force are not challenged. An example of individualization is an article entitled "OPP 'Killing Machine' Blamed in Man's Death," in the *Toronto Star* in 1988. The story was about a man who was killed in his back yard by a ten-man tactical team. Throughout the article the officers were accused of wrongful activity and illegitimate actions, but the article never implicated the Ontario Provincial Police institution. The article alluded to the fact that the ten officers acted outside the rules of accepted behaviour, but the purpose and duties of tactical teams was not mentioned. Although the men acted in accordance with their training and outlined procedures, they were held individually accountable.

In much of the press coverage involving such incidents the stories are presented as decontextualized, individualized personal experiences, without a focus on the systemic flaws within the policing institution. For example, the June 27, 1995 *Gazette* editorial about the verdict for the five officers, "Justice Is Done in Barnabé Verdict," stated that "the rest of us can find comfort in justice having been served. The jury's verdict seems fair," assumed something about the entire Montreal community, especially since sentences had not yet been handed down. The editorial stated that the five officers were considering an appeal. Even though the officers faced a maximum ten-year prison term, the Crown was not expected to ask for jail sentences. The *Gazette* editor would be satisfied if the officers were fired. This disciplinary measure might satisfy the editor, but it would not necessarily appease all Montrealers. The editorial individualized and depoliticized the behaviour of the implicated officers as bad apples without implicating the policing institution within which they were trained and worked. The article ended

> Most police officers are committed to doing a first-class job. And Montrealers admire them for the professionalism and dedication with which they do their very difficult jobs.... Their lives are sometimes endangered and often, they must make life-and-death decisions in a split second. Officers work under stressful conditions and can make honest mistakes.[20]

There was no mention of the fatal shooting of Martin Suazo and other mishandled and/or unjustified incidents. The editorial stated that the verdict had helped to restore public confidence in the criminal justice system's response to police excesses.

The Barnabé trial coverage created sympathy for the MUC police officers who had been criminally indicted for the reduced charge of assault causing bodily harm, with sentences of probation and either weekend jail terms or community service. This sympathy was misdirected; ordinary citizens accused of a similar crime are treated differently. The reports on the fatal shooting of Martin Suazo presented him as a troubled youth whose delinquency caused his death, even though the circumstances surrounding his death—being shot in the head while lying on the ground waiting to be handcuffed—made the shooting completely unjustified. The negative coverage of the SQ also diverted attention away from the Montreal force and were aimed at diminishing its responsibility for unacceptable and unjustified brutality.

The print media is an important institution when police abuses are being considered because it is a significant disseminator of information. Social control institutions, including the police, make use of the media to redefine questionable events, pacify citizen allegations, and maintain their legitimacy. The mainstream print media presents a particular reality as objective fact to the public while maintaining a public position of objectivity and impartiality. The media accepts as given that our communities need police protection at any price, even if the cost is our lives.

CHAPTER FOUR

In Memory of the Victims

There has been tremendous controversy in Montreal and Toronto in recent years about shootings of blacks by the police. The black communities in both cities are outraged and have vehemently expressed their concerns that blacks are targeted and killed by the police. Many accuse the policing institution as a whole of being trigger happy towards their communities. Racism defines the debate.

Dan Philip, president of the Black Coalition of Quebec, has complained that "whenever the Police approach members of the Black community, they always come with their guns drawn and pointing."[1] The black community has also voiced concern over the high level of police discretionary power and lack of accountability when shooting deaths occur. Civil rights leader Eldridge Cleaver commented on this double standard in the 1960's: "The racist conscience of America is such that murder does not register as murder, really, unless the victim is white."[2] In Montreal and Toronto accountability is non-existant, regardless of race or circumstance.

There are several reports on police conduct, including the Bellemaire report regarding the death of Anthony Griffin, the Yarosky coroner's report regarding the death of Marcellus François, and the Lewis Report in Ontario. They all reveal that the police fail to take necessary precautions when the lives of citizens are in danger. They have also confirmed that a disproportionately large number of blacks have been killed by police officers in the two cities. Many blacks fear and distrust the police because they know that they are considered enemies.

The issue of police racism is at the forefront of political debate. The concerns of black community members in Montreal and Toronto must be addressed. The following section focuses on the official deaths caused by police in Montreal and Toronto between 1987 and 1993. Deaths caused by

MONTREAL DEATHS (1987-1993)		
Name	**Date**	**Race**
Anthony Griffin	Nov. 11, 1987	black
Jose Carlos Garcia	Oct. 7, 1988	hispanic
Yvon Lafrance	Jan. 3, 1989	white
Presley Leslie	Apr. 9, 1990	black
Jorge Chavarria	Nov. 22, 1990	hispanic
Paul McKinnon	Oct. 25, 1990	white
Marcellus Francois	Jul. 6, 1991	black
Armand Fernandez	Nov. 4, 1991	hispanic
Osmond Fletcher	Nov. 14, 1991	black
Trevor Kelly	Jan. 1, 1993	black
Yvon Asselin	Mar. 6, 1993	white

TORONTO DEATHS (1987-1993)		
Name	**Date**	**Race**
Eugene Desmarais	Oct. 19, 1987	white
Gardiner Myers	Jul. 9, 1988	white
Lester Donaldson	Oct. 7, 1988	black
Wade Lawson	Dec. 8, 1988	black
Mark Ageoili	Nov. 4, 1989	white
Donald Peltier	Jan. 25, 1990	black
Joseph Boisjoly	Dec. 26, 1990	white
Kenneth Allen	Nov. 29, 1991	black
Raymond Lawrence	May 2, 1992	black
Dominic Sabatino	Aug. 9, 1992	white
Luis Vega	Dec. 26, 1992	hispanic
Ian Coley	Apr. 20, 1993	black

Individuals killed by police in Montreal and Toronto, 1987-1993.

Montreal and Toronto police between 1994-1997 appear in Appendix 2.

Of the eleven killings in Montreal five victims were black, three were hispanic, and three were white. In 1991 Montreal had a total population of 3,091,115, 38,650 of whom were black (1.25 % of the population);[3] a disproportionately high number of visible minorities have been killed by the police in Montreal. All of the victims, except Paul McKinnon, were killed by police officers using handguns.

Of the twelve deaths in Toronto, six victims were black, one was hispanic and five were white. Although an equal number of whites and blacks were killed by the police, the black population is a much smaller percentage of the population. In 1991, of Toronto's total population of 3,863,105, only 125,610 were black (3.25 percent of the population).[4] Most of the deaths were caused by police officers using handguns, but Gardiner Myers was beaten to death, and Mark Ageoili died in a car crash during a police chase.

Individual killings fall within several categories:

<u>Accidental or Non-Accidental Deaths</u>

Accidental deaths are shootings which are unintentional and which the police allege are a mistake.

Non-accidental deaths are shootings which are intentional where the police acknowledge that they used necessary force to protect themselves or the public. Whether or not the victim was armed or type of weapon.

<u>Motive for Shooting</u>

Fleeing felon: to prevent a suspect from fleeing arrest.

Public safety: to preserve the lives of citizens.

Self-defence: to preserve the life of the officer.

A Summary of Incidents in Montreal and Toronto

A brief description of the incident and shooting, including contradictory facts and details, and statements by witnesses, which contradict or challenge the officer's statements.

The outcome, whether or not the officer is exonerated, is also indicated.

This information has been extracted from the policing institutions' statements of events. The police perspective of the incidents is included to demonstrate that even their records confirm that many of the incidents causing death were unjustified.

Anthony Griffin: black (November 11, 1987)[5]
Death accidental; unarmed
Motive: Fleeing felon
He was shot once in the head during an apparent escape attempt even though he had obeyed the officer's order to halt. The officer alleged that his gun was cocked and fired accidently. The incident called into question the validity of the fleeing felon provision of the Criminal Code of Canada.
Contradictions and inconsistencies: The question of why the officer had cocked the gun if he had no intention of shooting, is raised.
Outcome: Officer exonerated

Jose Carlos Garcia: hispanic (October 7, 1988)[6]
Death non-accidental; armed (firearm)
Motive: Public-safety & self-defence
He was shot and killed for reportedly walking down a crowded downtown street carrying a firearm. Shots were fired after he had allegedly wounded an officer. A coroner's inquest concluded that the police firing on a crowded street was extremely hazardous to public safety.
Contradictions and inconsistencies: Witnesses stated that the police officer fired first.
Outcome: Officer exonerated

Yvon Lafrance: white (January 3, 1989)[7]
Death non-accidental
Armed (knife)
Motive: Self-defence
He was shot in the heart in his backyard after he allegedly lunged at officers with the knife. Officers were called because he allegedly chased his male companion out of the yard. He was drunk at the time of the incident.
Contradictions and inconsistencies: A witness stated that Lafrance made no attempt to approach the officers involved. Furthermore, in 1996, seven years after the incident, ex-Sûreté du Québec officer Gaetan Rivest, who had investigated the Lafrance case, admitted that evidence had been

fabricated to avoid holding the officer accountable. The victim was descibed as being four to ten feet away from the officer when shot, instead of fifteen to twenty-five feet as he was. Rivest stated that the officer shot Lafrance out of nervousness while Lafrance was moving further away from the officers.

Outcome: Officer exonerated

Presley Leslie: black (April 9, 1990)[8]

Death non-accidental

Armed (fiearm)

Motive: Public safety

He was shot in a downtown bar after firing a gun. The police arrived on the scene to find a man at the top of the stairs firing.

Contradictions and inconsistencies: A witness testified that Leslie only shot two bullets into the ceiling when he heard a song he liked. Other witnesses stated that he was not firing his gun in the bar before the police arrived.

Outcome: Officer exonerated

Paul McKinnon: white (October 25, 1990)[9]

Death accidental

Unarmed

The 14-year-old was run over by an officer who was responding to a radio call at high speed. The officer ran a red light and struck the youth in front of Concordia University's west-end campus.

Contradictions and inconsistencies: Constable Markovic received a 45-day jail sentence in 1995 for dangerous driving causing death because he failed to show remorse towards the victim's family. He later returned to duty.

Outcome: Officer convicted but on appeal.

Jorge Chavarria: hispanic (November 22, 1990)[10]

Death non-accidental

Armed (knife)

Motive: Fleeing felon and self-defence

He was shot and killed by an undercover officer while fleeing a Provi-Soir convenience store with a loaf of bread, cold cuts and eggs. He left the store without threatening the employee. He was shot after he allegedly lunged at the officer with a knife outside the store.

Contradictions and inconsistencies: A witness stated that Chavarria dropped the knife before the officer shot him.

Outcome: Officer exonerated

Marcellus François: black (July 6, 1991)[11]

Death accidental

Unarmed

No motive: police shot the wrong man

He was shot in the head while in his car by MUC Tactical Squad in a case of 'mistaken identity.' The police were searching for two murder suspects and there were three other persons in the car. François allegedly appeared to reach down and pull out what looked like a gun

Contradictions and inconsistencies: No weapon was found in the car. François was short, clean-shaven with short hair, while both suspects were over six feet tall, one with a beard and one with long hair. Only two police officers were suspended by the police ethics committee. One officer was suspended for 10 days for unjustifiably detaining the three other occupants of the car; the other was suspended for two days for searching the home of two suspects without a warrant.

Outcome: Officers exonerated

Armand Fernandez: hispanic (November 4, 1991)[12]

Death non-accidental

Armed (steak knife)

Motive: Fleeing felon and self-defence

He was fatally shot after a downtown chase which resulted in four damaged cars and five minor injuries to police officers. He allegedly lunged at an officer before he was shot. The vehicle had been reported stolen.

Contradictions and inconsistencies: What is the level of threat posed by a man with a steak knife to officers during a chase.

Outcome: Officer exonerated

Osmond Fletcher: black (November 14, 1991)[13]

Death accidental

Armed (firearm)

No motive: Police allege that he shot himself in the head following a chase and before the police could subdue him. He refused to stop when instructed to do so by the officers. The police were acting on a warrant for drug trafficking charges from the Toronto police department.

Contradictions and inconsistencies: Three witnesses stated that the police shot Fletcher. Affidavits indicated that he was left-handed, which contradicted the conclusions of the coroner's report which stated that he was shot in the right ear.

Outcome: Officer exonerated

Trevor Kelly: black (January 1, 1993)[14]

Death non-accidental

Armed (knife)

Motive: Self-defence

He was shot in the back because he allegedly held a knife and was moving aggressively towards an officer on a west-end street.

Contradictions and inconsistencies: Neighbours stated that the police visited Kelly in his apartment for approximately half an hour shortly before the shooting. A witness stated that Kelly was not carrying a knife. Another witness testified that Kelly saw the police and turned around to walk the other way but that they continued to drive slowly beside him. Why did the officers trail Kelly in their car after he left home on foot?

Outcome: Officers exonerated

Yvon Asselin: white (March 6, 1993)[15]

Death non-accidental

Armed (knife)

Motive: Public safety

The police SWAT team shot a man with rubber bullets after responding to a call from a woman who reported that she had been threatened. Asselin was brandishing a knife in his apartment and slammed the door on the officers when they ordered him to surrender.

Contradictions and inconsistencies: The coroner concluded that the cause of death was unknown. The use of rubber bullets remained unchallenged.
Outcome: Officers exonerated

The police acknowledged that only two of the eleven individuals killed by the police in Montreal were unarmed black men, Anthony Griffin and Marcellus François. In both cases there was clear evidence of the misuse of deadly force but all of the officers involved were absolved of any criminal responsibility. The incidents were deemed accidental because of a malfunctioning firearm which accidentally discharged in the case of Anthony Griffin, and of mistaken identity in the case of Marcellus François. The death of Osmond Fletcher, also black, was also determined to be accidental based on the police statement that he shot himself being accepted by the coroner. Only three of the eleven, one hispanic and two blacks, had firearms. The remaining five were armed with knives. Are people armed with knives as dangerous as those with firearms, and is killing them the only way to subdue them?

TORONTO INCIDENTS

Eugene Desmarais: white (October 19, 1987)[16]
Death non-accidental
Armed (knife)
Motive: Fleeing felon
He was shot in the heart during a high speed police chase after fleeing a robbery scene. When the officer ordered him to drop the knife, he ran towards an empty cab.
Contradictions and inconsistencies: none available
Outcome: Officer exonerated

Gardiner Myers: white (July 9, 1988)[17]
Death accidental
Unarmed
Motive: Self Defence
He died in his cell shortly after being arrested by Metro Toronto police on suspicion of burglary charges. He had apparently fought with four officers,

during which one officer admitted to hitting him with a nightstick at least six times before he was finally subdued. Autopsy indicated that his lungs had filled with fluid which caused him to drown.

Contradictions and inconsistencies: The coroner stated that the injuries suffered by Myers as a result of the beating played no part in his death. Yet his report also revealed that a cluster of puncture-type abrasions indicating forceful contact and bruising were found on twenty-five different areas of his body.

Outcome: Officers exonerated

Lester Donaldson: black (October 7, 1988)[18]
Death non-accidental
Armed (knife)
Motive: Self-defence
Donaldson, mentally ill, was shot after the police were called to investigate a complaint at a rooming house. The police allegedly saw him threatening four people with a knife which he also allegedly swung at the officers when they attempted to detain him.

Contradictions and inconsistencies: He had been shot five months earlier by Metro Toronto officers in another incident and remained partially paralysed due to the injury. Although there were serious discrepancies in the testimony of the five officers questioned, the implicated officer was absolved at the criminal trial.

Outcome: Officer exonerated

Wade Lawson: black (December 8, 1988)[19]
Death non-accidental
Unarmed
Motive: Fleeing felon
He was shot in the back of the head as he and a companion fled from the police in a stolen car. The police shot at the rear window as the stolen car sped away. Six shots were fired by police.

Contradictions and inconsistencies: Police first said that he was shot as he drove a stolen car towards them but later admitted that the shot was fired from behind the car.

Outcome: Officers exonerated

Mark Ageoili: white (November 4, 1989)[20]
Death accidental
Unarmed
No motive: He died in a car crash during a police chase. He was killed and three others teenagers were injured when their stolen car crashed into a concrete construction barrier as they were being chased by the police. The car had travelled two kilometres before crashing. The other youths were charged with possession of stolen property.
Contradictions and inconsistencies. Due to the short distance travelled, the police did not technically call it a chase, and were thus absolved of any responsibility.
Outcome: Officers exonerated

Donald Peltier: black (January 25, 1990)[21]
Death non-accidental
Armed (firearm)
Motive: Self-defence
He was fatally shot after he ran from a bullet-ridden car following a high-speed chase. The police allege that he and his partners had shot out the back window of the car and had commenced firing at the police vehicle. There were two other black suspects in the car.
Contradictions and inconsistencies: none available
Outcome: Officers exonerated

Joseph Boisjoly: white (December 26, 1990)[22]
Death non-accidental
Armed (replica handgun)
Motive: Self-defence
Police arrived on the scene after they received a call about a drunken man who was firing a gun in the area. The police opened fire when Boisjoly refused to drop his weapon after allegedly pointing it at them. Boisjoly was shot dead after firing five blanks from a replica handgun.
Contradictions and inconsistencies: The handgun was later examined to establish

whether or not it had been modified to fire real bullets. It was concluded that the handgun had not been modified and had only fired blanks.

Outcome: Officers exonerated

Kenneth Alfonso Allen: black (November 29, 1991)[23]

Death non-accidental

Unarmed

Motive: unknown

Subdued and handcuffed by police after he allegedly attacked a streetcar driver. While on the way to the station, Allen was rushed to a hospital where he died of an alleged cocaine overdose, 77 minutes after he was taken into custody.

Contradictions and inconsistencies: The media had reported little about Allen's death because it was originally ruled as a cocaine overdose. The SIU re-opened the case three years later due to new evidence which showed that Allen had bruising on his neck which suggested that the police had used excessive force. The officer involved, Constable Van Seters, was charged with two counts of criminal negligence and refused to cooperate with the SIU. An inquest into the matter was abruptly cancelled in early 1994 without explanation.

Outcome: Officer exonerated

Raymond Lawrence: black (May 2, 1992)[24]

Death non-accidental

Armed (knife)

Motive: Fleeing Felon and self-defence

Lawrence, a suspected drug dealer, was shot twice in the chest after a long foot chase. The police allege that he pulled a knife on one of the officers.

Contradictions and inconsistencies: The family's lawyer stated that the officer's view may have been blocked by a fence when he said he saw Lawrence run at another officer with a knife before being fatally shot. The officer involved in the shooting admitted that his notes were sketchy and that they did not mention the knife.

Outcome: Officer exonerated

Dominic Sabatino: white (August 9, 1992)[25]
Death non-accidental
Armed (baseball bat)
Motive: Self-defence
He was shot in the abdomen after allegedly threatening two officers with the bat. The officers fired a warning shot into the ground and then one of the officers shot him from one metre away as he attempted to raise the bat He had been chasing his brother out of their mother's home. He was mentally disturbed and had apparently stopped taking his medication for schizophrenia.
Contradictions and inconsistences: The family, who were present at the time of the shooting, urged the police not to shoot him. They told the officers that he was not feeling well and that he needed help.
Outcome: Officer exonerated

Luis Vega: hispanic (December 26, 1992)[26]
Death non-accidental
Armed (butcher knife)
Motive: Self-defence
He was shot three times and killed in his apartment by police after having a drunken argument with his wife and brother. He apparently ran towards the officers with the butcher knife.
Contradictions and inconsistencies: The officer involved refused to cooperate with the Special Investigations Unit, an external review board in Ontario which investigates deaths caused by the police.
Outcome: Officer exonerated

Ian Coley: black (April 20, 1993)[27]
Death non-accidental
Armed (firearm)
Motive: Fleeing felon and self-defence
He was pulled over in what the police believed was a stolen car and then was chased by foot; shot in the chest twice and killed. The police allege that he fired first. Before the shooting incident the police had followed him and witnessed a transaction involving firearms.

Contradictions and inconsistencies: It was later found that the car was not stolen. One of the officers involved refused to cooperate with the external review board. The investigation concluded that the victim's gun had not been fired. At the inquest into the shooting, the jury did not make any recommendations that adressed how the death could have been prevented but instead focused on the expansion of the Metro Toronto Black Organized Crime Squad.

Outcome: Officers exonerated

Of the twelve Toronto incidents, the police acknowledged that four of the individuals were unarmed, two victims were white and two were black. Gardiner Myers was not killed with a firearm, but was beaten in a cell and subsequently died. Mark Ageoili was killed in a car crash during a police chase. Kenneth Allen's death was originally deemed a cocaine overdose, but the case was later re-opened because of bruising found on his neck. Wade Lawson, the only unarmed individual who was killed by a firearm, was shot in the back of the head while fleeing. Only two of the twelve were allegedly armed with guns, Donald Peltier and Ian Coley. Of the remaining, four were armed with knives, one with a baseball bat and one with a replica firearm. Only two of the twelve deaths were judged accidental. Gardiner Myers, whom both the police and the coroner maintain did not die as a result of the beating, and Mark Ageoili, who was killed in a car crash which was not defined as a chase. Two of the twelve individuals killed, Lester Donaldson and Dominic Sabatino, were mentally ill.

In all of the shooting incidents the police were absolved of all criminal responsibility regardless of the circumstances, except for the officer responsible for the death of Paul McKinnon. Some of the circumstances of the cases challenge the exoneration of the officers involved and the policing system's lack of accountability. Even in the cases of deaths deemed accidental the officers were not held responsible. If, for example, a citizen causes an accidental death in a bar brawl, s/he will usually be indicted on at least a manslaughter charge, however, in the case of a police officer contributing to the death of an individual, apparently another standard is applied.

The majority of the people killed were not armed with guns—five of the 23; or with knives—nine of the 23 were, or a replica firearm—one of the 23, or with a baseball bat—one of the 23. A total of 19 of 23 victims were killed with police firearms. Is lethal force using firearms considered necessary in cases where individuals are armed with knives or baseball bats? Many would say that it is excessive or unjustified.

A review of the incidents involving deaths at the hands of police in Montreal and Toronto between 1987 to 1993 strongly suggests that many deaths occurred under questionable circumstances, especially when the victim was black. There are incidents of seeming police overreaction when dealing with blacks, as in the cases of Anthony Griffin, Marcellus François and Wade Lawson, which suggest that the black population is perceived by the police as being a greater threat than the white population. Although blacks are not the majority of people killed by police—eleven of 23—the percentage far surpasses their proportion of the population in both cities. In addition, in these 23 cases, four were hispanic or other people of colour, for a total of 14 members of some visible minority group, or approximately 61% of those who were killed.

A disproportionate number of blacks are killed by the police in both Montreal and Toronto often under questionable circumstances, which has led many to accuse the police of racism. If we accept that racism exists in our society, then we also know that policing institutions, which are a part of our society, are not exempt. Policing is a sector where racism is amplified because of the power and control vested in law officers. Racial discrimination affects how police officers conduct themselves with individuals from various ethnic communities in the commission of their duties.

Although police racism affects people of all visible minority groups, it is most pronounced against the black community. Racism has been at the core of black history in North America since blacks were transported from Africa as slaves. The black population is, de facto, considered dangerous. In 1911 Canadian government officials used the fact that the black inmate population in the United States was higher than the white population to ban black immigration into Canada.[28] It is this element which continues to legitimize the extreme police response of physical force.

It may be that members of black communities in Canada and in the United States provide convenient 'scapegoats primarily because they are considered a threat. There is a particular belief within the policing institution and among its officers about which groups are responsible for committing street crimes—that more blacks commit street crimes—so police officers are more suspicious of them. Police officers are more likely to police areas where there is a large black population because they consider them to be high crime areas. Any area where more police are present provokes more apprehension, regardless of actual threat being posed. This, in turn, leads to more arrests,[29] which further legitimizes the police institution's increased allocation of resources and manpower to these specific areas. This directs attention away from the stereotypes that are inherently racist and which set blacks apart from the rest of society. A lawyer at the inquest into the shooting of Ian Coley, a young black man in Toronto, also suggests that there is an extra layer of policing for the black communities. For example, Metro-Toronto police's black organized crime squad is aimed specifically at investigating crimes committed by blacks.[30] Members of the squad firmly believe that their unit is necessary to protect the black community from themselves and thus merits expansion. Detective Davis McLeod, a member of the Black Organized Crime Squad said, "Gunmen... are only a small percentage. Operations such as these have a great bearing on the safety of the black community."[31]

Police officers, because they operate within a larger institutional context, cannot be examined in isolation. They must be viewed from within the context of institutional racism where blacks are considered a policing problem at the institutional level. The police are part of a racist society and cases like Anthony Griffin's are part of a long history of racially-motivated brutality.

CHAPTER FIVE

The Allan Gosset Case

"In no way am I racist. Where I used to live in Lasalle, there were many black people and I often vacation in countries that are predominantly black."

Gosset's response at a hearing when accused
of racism. *Montreal Gazette*, April 21, 1988

The 1987 killing of Anthony Griffin by MUC police constable Allan Gosset has become a symbol of the racism and police brutality directed against the black community in Montreal. Police officials maintain that it was a catalyst for change and improvement within the MUC police force. The killing ignited the police racism controversy and crystallized the various debates and positions of the government, the police, the courts, and the black community. Because the Gosset case involved various criminal and disciplinary proceedings it provides a basis for a discussion of the various legal channels available when a killing incident occurs as well as an evaluation of their effectiveness. The discussion includes information about the disciplinary and court proceedings, the policing institution's refusal to acknowledge responsibility, and the exclusive rights of police officers involved in shooting incidents.

THE INCIDENT

On November 11, 1987 Anthony Griffin, a 19-year-old unarmed black man, was shot once in the head in Nôtre-Dame-de-Grâce by Constable Allan Gosset of the Montreal Urban Community police. The 16-year veteran shot and killed Griffin during an alleged escape attempt outside Station 15 in Côte-des-Neiges. He had previously been approached by two officers for refusing to pay a cab fare. The officers ran a computer check and discovered that there was an outstanding warrant for his arrest on a breaking and entering charge. They decided to bring him to the station. He was unarmed, but had not been searched or handcuffed before being brought to the station. In the station parking lot Griffin allegedly attempted to escape on foot and was ordered to halt by Gosset and his partner Kim Campbell. He had obeyed the order and had turned around but was shot in the forehead from a distance of approximately six metres. He died a few hours later in hospital.

The Police Account

From the beginning Allan Gosset stated that the shooting was an accident. He claimed that he pointed his firearm, which he did not know was cocked, at Griffin to intimidate him into complying, and it malfunctioned and fired accidently. MUC police chief Roland Bourget suspended Gosset without pay pending an investigation because Griffin had obeyed the order to halt and was facing Gosset when shot. Bourget told the press that, according to the MUC police directives, police officers were only allowed to shoot a suspect when a life is endangered, but not to stop a suspect from fleeing. From the outset the chief geared attention towards why Gosset pointed his gun in the first place. Bourget stated "The policeman, according to information I have, was pointing his firearm and a shot went off, hitting (the suspect) in the head." Bourget denied all allegations that the shooting of the black youth was the result of racism, "I am personally convinced that this act is not related to racism, the same incident would have happened if the person was Asian, black or white."[1]

Although Gosset was suspended without pay, immediately after the incident he began receiving workers' compensation benefits covering 90 percent of his $380 weekly salary for one year because of the nervous shock he suffered as a result of the killing.[2]

Past History

In 1981 Allan Gosset had been involved in the beating of a 36-year-old black man, Daniel Otchere, whom he allegedly called a 'damn nigger.' Otchere was stopped in his car by Gosset and his partner and asked for identification, which he willingly provided. Gosset then ordered him, in French, to turn off the motor and to keep the door shut. Otchere, who had difficulty understanding French, tried to open the car door and at this point the officers began beating him. Otchere stated that Gosset told him, "If you don't get out of the car, damned nigger, I'll hit you in the eye."[3] Otchere sustained a broken nose and the loss of eyesight for two weeks as a result of the beating. He was hit in the stomach, shoulder and legs with a flashlight by Gosset and the other officer and was held in a cell overnight before being released.

He complained to the MUC Police Complaints Review Board, but the case was rejected. He then presented his case to the Quebec Police Commission, which reprimanded Gosset for the use of excessive force. No disciplinary action was taken against him. Otchere sued the MUC for $8,100 but agreed to a $2,450 out-of-court settlement. In 1983 the Human Rights Commission concluded that the arrest was legal but ruled that excessive force had been used.[4] Although race may have played a role, Chief Roland Bourget denied any link between the 1981 incident and the killing of Griffin. He maintained that the shooting was not racially motivated and that it might have been a coincidence that both incidents involved blacks. At a news conference he stated, "I cannot believe, maybe I'm naive, that the police will shoot someone because they're black."[5]

BLACK COMMUNITY RESPONSE

Three hundred mourners attended Anthony Griffin's funeral in Montreal. The black community was outraged and accused police officers of frequently getting off the hook in incidents involving black killings. The executive director of the Black Community Council of Quebec sent a statement to the media stating that the black community would not be satisfied until Gosset was charged with murder. He asked, "Why was the gun aimed at the head of the youth at 16 feet, when the regulation stipulates that the gun should never have left his holster, unless to protect the life of an officer or that of a citizen?"[6]

The police chief voiced his concerns over the reputation of the MUC force after the shooting incident. In response to the allegations, he used the bad apple analogy, that the entire force did not deserve the racist label because one of its officers had killed a black man. He also denied responsibility for the hiring practices of the MUC regarding visible minorities, stating, "When I came here three years ago, there was one black policeman. Now there are six...That's a 600 percent improvement."[7] The MUC police force employed over 4500 officers in 1987, six were from the black community.

On direct orders from Quebec Justice Minister Claude Ryan a manslaughter charge was laid on November 20, 1987 against Gosset. It caused considerable controversy. Black community leaders believed that the charge should have been murder, and stated that the lesser charge was to be expected because it is the police who police the police. They also commented that an involuntary homicide charge could not be valid because Griffin was unarmed.

On November 21, 1987 over 2000 members of the black community protested against the reduced charge. A contributing factor which led to the protest was that Gosset had not been placed under formal arrest. Similar rallies were held in Quebec City, Toronto and Vancouver. Placards at the protests read: "Arrest Gosset for Murder Now," "Don't Shoot Please", "Who Polices the Police?," and "If Those Who Protect Us Kill Us, Then Who Will Protect Us?"[8] The protests obliged the Minister of Cultural Communities and Immigration to call for a royal commission into racism within Quebec's police forces; it did not refer to the Griffin incident directly, but to recently publicized events.[9]

The Preliminary Hearing

On December 22, 1987 Judge Bernard Bilodeau, in a two-day preliminary hearing, found no evidence of racism linked to the Griffin incident; but he did order Gosset to stand trial for manslaughter. At the hearing Gosset's partner, Kim Campbell, testified that she believed that the shot went off unexpectedly because she did not hear the click of the hammer. This suggested that the gun was cocked before it was taken out of the holster.[10] Shooting instructor Michel Menard also testified and supported Campbell, stating that it was unlikely but possible that the gun was cocked before it left the holster. Another officer who witnessed the shooting testified that Gosset was in shock after the shooting.[11]

After the hearing Gosset said he was relieved and felt much better that the incident had not been linked to racism. His lawyer, Serge Menard (who later became the Quebec Public Security Minister), criticized the MUC

Police, claiming that they contributed to the overall atmosphere of guilt by suspending Gosset without pay. Griffin's father, Orberth Griffin, told reporters that he remained convinced that racism caused the shooting. "If it was a white person, he (Gosset) would not have pulled a gun or shot."[11]

THE TRIAL

The criminal trial began on February 15, 1988 with the Crown forwarding the charge of an *unlawful act manslaughter*. The argument was that the act of pointing his revolver constituted Gosset's careless handling of a firearm and was contrary to Section 86(2) of the Criminal Code,[12] which states that anyone handling a firearm in a careless manner without taking safety precautions is guilty of an indictable offence with a maximum prison sentence of two years. The Crown was thus required to prove that Gosset's handling of the firearm was careless relative to what is expected of a police officer under similar circumstances, and that Griffin's death was the result of Gosset's carelessness.

At the trial Gosset testified that his gun was accidently cocked when he removed it from his holster, and that he had no recollection of cocking it himself. In his written report, submitted following the shooting incident, Gosset had acknowledged that he might have cocked his firearm. When questioned by the prosecution about the written report, Gosset responded,

> Because when writing a report and... as the shot went off even though I had not made any decision to fire, I never made that decision. I attempted to explain how that happened. I could only explain that... that in taking my gun out while running, I would have cocked the gun, I would have armed (cocked) it without realizing it. I was running after him, I was shouting at him, and I was only concentrated on Anthony Griffin at that point in time.[13]

Gosset's main defence was his lack of recollection. He testified that he was not aware that the revolver was cocked and that he could not recall putting any pressure on the trigger. He also testified that he was not racist and did not intend to fire at Griffin. Gosset told the jurors that drawing the revolver "intimidates the suspect and it's a measure of protection for you."[14] MUC police directives do not allow officers to draw their guns to intimidate the public. Because of the 'Fleeing Felon' provision in the Criminal Code, the court agreed that Gosset was justified in taking out his gun to convince Griffin not to flee.[15]

Ballistic experts called by the prosecution stated that Gosset's firearm could not have fired accidently even if it was defective because its two mechanical safety features would have prevented firing. A series of experiments with Gosset's revolver in the courtroom confirmed it. The prosecution also argued that Gosset should not have had his finger on the trigger, but rather the trigger guard, if he intended only to intimidate Griffin. The trial judge dismissed this argument because the court did not know whether this stipulation was part of MUC police procedures.[16] When the prosecution attempted into admit in evidence MUC directives concerning the use of firearms, it was not permitted to do so because the judge believed that the 'administrative codified norm' for a given circumstance is not applicable in every circumstance and would thus render the evidence inconclusive.[17] The judge stated that police procedures could not be used to prove carelessness on Gosset's part because they could not apply in every situation. The trial judge inferred that police officers are not obliged to strictly follow directives if they believe that another course of action is necessary in a given circumstance. The assumption is that because police officers are specialized knowers, they can best decide how to conduct their duties.

In his charge to the jury the judge stated that in order for the *unlawful act manslaughter* charge to be upheld, Gosset had to have displayed a criminal state of mind—as opposed to mere negligence—at each stage of the incident. In his conclusion the judge asked the jury to consider the following five questions before reaching a verdict:

> Firstly, at the beginning of the incident, was there anything in the evidence which indicated a criminal state of mind on the part of the accused? Second, during the trip to the station, even after having learned other information such as the existence of a warrant for his arrest, and the fact that the young man was considered violent, did the evidence show this criminal state of mind on the part of

the accused? Third, upon their arrival to the station, before the attempted escape, was there anything in the evidence indicating a criminal state of mind on the part of the accused? Fourth, during the attempted escape, when the shot was fired, did the evidence show facts which could lead to the conclusion that the accused had, there again, a guilty state of mind? Fifth, immediately after the shot was fired, was the accused's attitude that of a person who showed a guilty state of mind or wanton or reckless disregard for the life of another person?"[18]

This guilty, or criminal, state of mind referred to Gosset's general state of mind throughout the incident rather than to the degree of his negligence in using his weapon in the parking lot. The judge's statement to the jury implied that in order to find Gosset guilty of the careless handling of a firearm the jury would have to conclude that he had a criminal mind and to have been negligent in his conduct from his initial encounter with Griffin until the shooting. The judge's second point focused on the outstanding warrant for breaking and entering, implying that Griffin should have automatically been considered to be violent, inferring that drawing the revolver was acceptable. He did not mention that Gosset did not perceive Griffin to be a threat, and had neither searched nor handcuffed him.

After the jury retired the prosecutor complained to the Superior Court Judge that he had increased the burden on the Crown to prove criminal intent, even though it was not necessary for the charge of an *unlawful act manslaughter*. For such a charge, the dangerous and reckless use of a firearm would be sufficient for a guilty verdict with no need to prove Gosset had a criminal state of mind.[19] This argument was dismissed by the trial judge.

On February 24, 1988, after 15 hours of deliberation, an all-white jury of seven women and five men found Gosset not guilty of manslaughter. The fact that there were no black jurors again begs the question of racism. After his acquittal a teary-eyed Gosset addressed the television cameras, "I had ten seconds to judge what it took my peers 15 hours to decide…You see the difference in the time we policemen have to act." If, as he asserted, his gun fired accidently due to technical problems and a faulty memory, what, exactly, did he need to judge and decide within those ten seconds?

He further stated, "(Griffin) was not the only victim in this event…there are his parents and there is myself and there is my family as well."[20] The black community was outraged at the acquittal. Gloria Augustus, Griffin's mother, was devastated by the not guilty verdict and asked, "If it had been you or me, an ordinary civilian, would we get off like that?… It's because he's a policeman that he got off." [21]

Apart from the obvious question of why Gosset felt the need to draw his gun when there was no apparent danger to life, two other important issues were not addressed at trial. First, why did Gosset need to draw his gun to prevent an escape when the facts demonstrated that he did not perceive Griffin to be dangerous? He did not search or handcuff Griffin, suggesting that Gosset did not believe he was armed. Why was Griffin not allowed to escape and be picked up later? Secondly, if Gosset merely drew his gun to scare Griffin, why was the gun aimed at his head? He aimed well; Griffin was shot in the forehead from six metres.

After the acquittal MUC Police Chief Bourget maintained Gosset's suspension until the MUC disciplinary proceedings were concluded. This caused a conflict between the administration and the police brotherhood—the police union. The brotherhood publicly accused their chief of scapegoating Gosset to appease the black community. Bourget also denied any and all institutional responsibility for the shooting of Griffin, stating that "Anthony Griffin was not killed by an entire police department. He was killed by one man." The police union president, Louis Simard, stated that the MUC's refusal to return Gosset to duty after his acquittal had caused front-line officers to seriously question the force's support. He told reporters that "Police right now are worried… they don't know if they have protection in their activities as policemen. If you don't know you have that protection, you ask yourself questions (but) when you're in action, if you hesitate on something, it means that the policeman may be shot."[22] The implication is that police officers should have the force's protection regardless of circumstances.

The Quebec Police Commission

In April 1988 Gosset appeared before a provincial police disciplinary board to justify his conduct during the shooting incident. The Quebec Police

Commission was investigating Gosset's conduct and state of mind when he shot and killed Griffin. More than twenty witnesses were called to testify to help determine whether any additional disciplinary action should be taken. At the hearing Gosset once again stated that his gun was unknowingly cocked and that it fired accidently. He also testified that he usually relied on his own judgement rather than strictly adhering to MUC police procedures regarding body searches and the use of handcuffs. He added that he did not search and handcuff Griffin because he had not resisted arrest and therefore did not appear to be dangerous, showed no signs of aggression, and was very co-operative and very polite. Gosset also adamantly denied allegations that he had made racist comments prior to the shooting. He said, "In no way am I racist. Where I used to live in Lasalle, there were many black people and I often vacation in countries that are predominantly black."[23] For him, living among blacks is an unusual and commendable act. In refuting allegations of racism, Gosset's lawyer argued that one symptom of racism is suspicion and yet Gosset trusted Griffin enough not to search or handcuff him. He stated, "If he had been suspicious, damn it, none of this ever would have happened." [24] Was this intended to encourage police suspicion against blacks to avoid possible firearm malfunctions?

A ballistics expert testified that Gosset's firearm could not have gone off accidently as had been stated. Gosset's service revolver was repeatedly thrown to the ground in order to demonstrate that even with the hammer cocked it would not fire. The expert told the commission that the firearm was in perfect firing condition, and would only fire when pressure was exerted on the trigger. Before the proceedings, he had tested the firearm in the lab by cocking the hammer 1,115 times to determine whether it would slip back into place by itself, but it stayed cocked every time. He further stated that even if the firearm had become cocked by itself, its two mechanical safety features would have prevented it from firing. Based primarily on this ballistics evidence, in June 1988 the Quebec Police Commission found Gosset negligent and careless in the use of his firearm and recommended that the force dismiss him. The commission was satisfied that racism played no part in the shooting. Gosset was criticized for not having searched or handcuffed Griffin, as well as for pointing his firearm without justification. The commission made six recommendations.[25]

1) Gosset should be dismissed.

2) MUC officers should be equipped with double action revolvers which require more force to squeeze the trigger.

Even though the commission concluded that Gosset was negligent and reckless and that the firearm was not inoperative, by making this recommendation they tacitly supported Gosset's claim that his firearm had malfunctioned. Although a ballistics expert refuted Gosset's claim that his revolver had been accidently cocked, the commission still recommended that the MUC be supplied with safer firearms.

3) Investigations of deaths in police custody should be investigated by a different force, namely the Sûreté du Québec.

Prior to the Gosset case, all deaths had been investigated internally by the MUC police.

4) Suspects who seem suicidal or violent or who have escaped custody should be handcuffed while being transported.

This recommendations implied that Griffin was violent, even though Gosset admitted that he was polite and compliant.

5) Police should preserve all tapes of radio transmissions made during operations where deaths occur until all inquiries are completed.

The tape in the Griffin incident was erased before the commission's inquiry, so allegations that Gosset made racist comments prior to the shooting could not be proved.

6) The force should improve the physical fitness of its officers and ensure that all directives on police conduct are followed.

Although the Commission made these recommendations, the final decision would be made by the MUC disciplinary board and the MUC police chief.

MUC Police Disciplinary Board

The MUC board also concluded that Gosset had used unjustified force and had pointed his firearm without justification. Based on recommendations made by the MUC police disciplinary board on June 30, 1988 Chief Roland Bourget fired Gosset from the MUC police on July 8, 1988. Bourget told reporters that he had the power to confirm or annul the recommendations but decided to support the decision because of the seriousness of the incident and the degree of negligence on the part of the officer. He further stated that the media's coverage of the incident was exaggerated and dismissed all allegations of racism.

> Since the very beginning, I have never believed that this terrible accident was the result of racism. My belief and my position are the same today. There's no doubt in my mind that my decision would have been the same regardless of the sex or the race of the victim and regardless of any pressure that this might make... But today I'm saying that... I still feel this was not a racial incident. Gosset's shot could have missed Griffin and hit a police officer.... because I don't think he took aim and shot deliberately at Griffin. If that were the case he would have been found guilty in the criminal courts, which he wasn't.[26]

The chief continued to deny racism, which directed attention away from the organization's accountability. The decision to dismiss Gosset precipitated an open display hostility by the police brotherhood towards their chief. They accused him of sacrificing Gosset as a scapegoat to appease the black community, and then released a short communique which stated that their chief fired Gosset for that reason.[27] The statement, signed by union president Yves Prud'Homme, read "The Brotherhood speaks for policemen and policewomen in vigorously and bitterly denouncing the treatment which has made a victim of Allan Gosset... An unfortunate accident cannot justify so draconian a measure to satisfy a certain few."[28] Fellow officers collected $12,000 in solidarity with Allan Gosset, whose workers' compensation would expire in November 1988. It was the first instalment in a fund expected to top $30,000. It was obvious that fellow officers condoned

Gosset's behaviour and would do anything in their power to absolve him of any responsibility. On November 3, 1988 Gosset choked back tears and told an assembly of co-workers and reporters that he would swallow his pride and accept the money along with a pine carving of his police badge. He said that "[t]he fight isn't over, but I hope it's never necessary to collect like this for another officer."[29]

On November 11, 1988, one year after the shooting, when Gloria Augustus and approximately 100 community members held a candlelight vigil outside Station 15, the police asked them to leave the parking lot. She commented on the $12,000 that Gosset was given by his fellow officers, "It's unfair and totally wrong, I think. It's like they are saying to him 'Congratulations for what you have done.' I think it is very sad and disgusting."[30]

Labour Arbitration Hearing

The MUC police brotherhood appealed Gosset's firing before a provincial labour arbitration board; a hearing to determine whether Gosset should be reinstated began on November 28, 1988. At the hearing MUC lawyer Jacques Audette presented evidence which confirmed that Gosset had been injured a number of times in the past while transporting prisoners. This issue was raised to demonstrate that Gosset should have understood the importance of being careful while transporting a suspect in custody.[31] This argument was irrelevant because it was discovered after the fact that Griffin had been unarmed. Questioning Gosset's prudence before the shooting incident served to reinforce the belief that had he properly searched and handcuffed Griffin, there would not have been a shooting. Griffin was shot after he had obeyed the order to halt and was posing no threat to either of the officers present.

Serge Ménard, Gosset's lawyer, suggested that Anthony Griffin caused his own death by inciting Gosset to point his gun at him. Ménard stated, "What killed Anthony Griffin was what he did when he turned around to face Gosset."[32] When Gosset ordered Griffin to halt, Ménard claimed that he turned around and hopped from side to side. He claimed that Gosset pointed his gun at Griffin because he believed that he was in danger. This new evidence had not been presented at any previous court proceeding, including the criminal trial. Gosset had previously testified that he took out his revolver immediately after Griffin attempted to flee, before Griffin turned around, suggesting that Griffin was perceived to be dangerous immediately following the attempted escape rather than when he allegedly started hopping from side to side. Ménard appeared to be fabricating a new piece of evidence to justify the killing. It is unclear why this contradiction in testimony was not contested by the MUC lawyer. Ménard also argued that the only mistake Gosset made was being too lenient in not anticipating an attempted escape.[33]

On August 24, 1989 the arbitration hearing ruled in Gosset's favour for reinstatement and ruled that Griffin's death was an accident that should not have cost Gosset his job. Judge Lussier ruled that losing an estimated $70,000 in back pay was enough punishment for the mistake. In his report Lussier wrote, "…it is difficult to conclude that a police officer is not justified in using his weapon to convince a runaway who is dodging back and forth in front of him to stop moving, submit to his arrest and give up the use of his weapon if he has one on him."[34] Aside from the fact that Judge Lussier equated Gosset's monetary losses with the loss of Griffin's life, the fact that Gosset received workers' compensation for a period of one year and received 90 percent of his salary as well as $12,000 from his fellow officers was not considered. The judge ordered the MUC to reinstate Gosset within ten days of the ruling. It was ruled that Gosset erred in the shooting of Griffin but that the error did not justify his firing. The judge did stipulate that Gosset was not to be assigned any job which required the possession of a firearm. Neither the new MUC Chief, Alain St. Germain, nor Griffin's mother was pleased with the decision. Although he also denied that the shooting was racially motivated, St. Germain voiced his displeasure, "Our conclusion is that we disagree completely with the decision of the arbitrator, especially on two things: the using of a firearm and the gravity of the consequences of the incident."[35] He discussed plans to appeal the decision and stated that the use of the service revolver in this particular case was not justified.

Montreal's black community launched a campaign of protest aimed at preventing Gosset from returning to work, and letters were sent to St. Germain demanding an appeal. On August 29, 1989, after the police chief recommended an appeal to the arbitrator's order for the reinstatement of Gosset, the police union accused him of using Gosset as a scapegoat for political purposes. The police brotherhood once again accused their chief of pacifying the black community at Gosset's expense. "The brotherhood finds it unfortunate that the directors of the service are sacrificing one of their policemen in the sole aim to prevent a deterioration of relations with the minorities."[36] In early November 1989 the court rejected the chief's appeal and Gosset remained on the force.

On November 16, 1989 Allan Gosset applied for early retirement from the police force because he believed that the incident left him unfit for duty. He requested a pension of 80 percent of his salary as a result of this unfit condition. His request for early retirement was granted pending review by the administrators in charge of the pension fund, which required that he undergo testing by their medical experts.[37] Pending a decision he returned to duty in the wiretapping section of the MUC, which kept him unarmed and away from the public. His position in the wiretapping section, although considered a demotion, was technically a promotion because of its specialized status. Gosset's application for early retirement was accepted by MUC officials on November 23, 1991; he received a pension of 80 percent of his salary.[38]

Civil Suit

Gloria Augustus, Griffin's mother, launched a civil suit in the Quebec Superior Court against Gosset for $2,040,000. She contended that the shooting of her son was racially motivated and claimed that Gosset "demonstrated acts of wanton and reckless disregard for the physical security of a member of the black community."[39] Her lawyer, Reevin Pearl, stated that he would seek "punitive and exemplary damages" under the Canadian Charter of Human Rights and Freedoms. Former MUC Police Chief Roland Bourget testified at the trial that he continued to believe that the incident was not racially motivated, that it was an accident. The MUC director of internal affairs also testified that he believed that it had been an accident. Judge Guthrie interrupted Augustus' lawyer during questioning of the ex-chief about relations between blacks and police, "It's no secret that race problems have existed for several centuries and it's not likely they'll go away tomorrow, but I'm concerned with one particular incident in which a young man was shot."[40]

On July 20, 1990 Gloria Augustus was awarded $14,795 for the wrongful death of her son. Judge Guthrie ruled that Gosset had indeed acted illegally and with unjustified force when he shot Griffin, but he was not guilty of racial discrimination. He ordered Gosset to pay $4,000 to both Gloria Augustus and Griffin's father, Orberth Griffin. Both Gosset and the MUC were ordered to pay $10,795 plus costs to Augustus and $3,795 plus costs to Griffin. The judge limited costs to 12 of the 22 trial days because he stated that he believed that Reevin Pearl had extended the proceedings unnecessarily. He justified his decision by taking into account the previous disciplinary actions and other monetary punishments against Gosset. "After considering all relevant criteria and prior jurisprudence, the court concludes that an award of $8,000 of exemplary damages is reasonable in the circumstances of the present case." The judge did not consider the workers' compensation and $12,000 from the police brotherhood which Gosset had received. Reevin Pearl stated that the ruling was a step backward for justice and human rights and that the amount awarded would not cover Augustus' legal costs.[41]

The Appeals

A year after Gosset's criminal acquittal the Crown submitted a request for an appeal, which pleased the black community. The basis for the Crown's appeal was twofold. First, the trial judge had misdirected the jury by focusing entirely on the Criminal Code definition of criminal negligence where criminal intent must be proved, as opposed to focusing on Gosset's careless use of a firearm. Secondly, the trial judge had refused to allow evidence contained in MUC police directives which outline conditions under which firearms may be used during an arrest, preventing the prosecutor from establishing the extent of Gosset's negligence.[42] The request for appeal was submitted in 1988, but it took three years before it was scheduled in the Quebec Court of Appeal. On May 24, 1991 Appeal Court Justice Melvin Rothman ruled that the trial judge had failed to adequately brief the jury on the key points about whether or not the shooting was reckless, and ordered a second trial.[43] He agreed, however, with the trial judge's refusal to allow MUC police directives to be accepted as evidence. The black community were elated with the news of a new trial.

Gosset's lawyer appealed the order for a new trial before the Supreme Court of Canada on June 18, 1991; but on September 9, 1993 the Court maintained the ruling which ordered a new trial. The Court indicated that the all white jury which had acquitted Gosset was improperly instructed by the trial judge. Madame Justice Beverley McLachin stated that it would not have been necessary to prove criminal intent, but only that "his conduct was a marked departure from the standard of care of a reasonably prudent person in the circumstances." She stated that it was a case "of a person who fails to take reasonable precautions in response to the duty that has been placed upon him or her, and should have taken; the breach of this duty is demonstrated by the risk of harm to which their conduct gives rise."[44]

The Second Trial

Allan Gosset was tried a second time six years after the shooting, on March 21, 1994, for the careless use of a firearm. At the new trial, because the Supreme Court had concluded that the trial judge had erred in increasing the prosecution's burden to proving criminal intent, the prosecution was required to demonstrate only that Gosset was negligent in the performance of his duties. Gosset had already admitted at his first trial that he had used his service revolver to intimidate a suspect who was running away from him. He had also admitted that there was nothing which led him to believe that Griffin was armed. Nonetheless, prosecutor Jacques Trudel focused entirely on the state of Gosset's firearm, as opposed to the reasons Gosset drew his gun in the first place. He called numerous witnesses specialized in the technical aspects of firearms and their use. Gosset's lawyer, Jean-Claude Hébert, took advantage of this strategy and focused primarily on the issue of the malfunctioning firearm. Hébert used the cross-examination of a prosecution witness, firearms expert Michel Ménard, to suggest the possibility that Griffin could have worn a hidden small firearm or knife without Gosset being aware of it, in an attempt to legitimize Gosset's actions.[45] Hébert's strategy was an attempt to blame the victim for his own fate while presenting Gosset's action as reasonable.

During the trial the issue of racism was again denied. Hébert asserted that

During the trial the issue of racism was again denied. Hébert asserted that the public was ill-informed and blamed the incident entirely on inoperative MUC firearms. On April 8, 1994 Allan Gosset was found not guilty at his second trial and the Griffin family was again devastated by another acquittal. Griffin's father said

> Gosset did something wrong, we all knew that. Gosset murdered my son. He used the law, he hid behind it. There's no way we could have gotten justice... I'm not a racist person but I believe that both juries did not give us justice and I'm going to say freely that I do not think white people can give justice to black people...I think in their hearts they just can't.[46]

The prosecutor did not appeal the verdict.

INTERNAL STRUGGLES

THE COURT SYSTEM

There were two problems in attempting to use the court system to deal with the Anthony Griffin shooting and other incidents involving police officers— the failure of the courts to address the issue of police racism, and the lack of impartiality on the part of judges and lawyers when prosecuting a police officer. The Gosset case exposed an unwillingness by the courts to acknowledge that racism might play a role in police action. Throughout the criminal and civil court proceedings the issue of race was dismissed. As a result the MUC policing organization's responsibility was never investigated. Because both the courts and the police are state-run agencies, when incidents such as the killing of Anthony Griffin occur the judgement is from within the system. The criminal justice system is organized so that there is no arms-length legal channel for excessive police behaviour to be judged. The courts appear reluctant to address allegations of racism within the policing organization because, by doing so, they would unavoidably cast a 'dark cloud' over the entire structure of the state. The police are a front-line instrument of the state and any acknowledgement that racism might exist within the policing organization would 'plant the seed' that it permeates the entire system.

prosecuting police officers. The adversarial nature of the court system becomes ineffective when police officers are involved. When ordinary citizens contravene the law they are tried and judged in an independent arena. This does not mean that the court system treats all accused fairly and equally, but that the accused is not intrinsically connected to the legal process. When police officers are charged for actions committed during the commission of their duties, they remain a part of the state, being tried by the state. There is no external venue for these cases to be tried, so all the individuals involved are members of the apparatus, regardless of the side they find themselves on, with an interest in maintaining the integrity of the state. This integrity could not be maintained if the conduct of police officers who are the front-line agents of the state were seriously questioned. It is not a true adversarial arrangement because everyone involved has a common interest, they are interchangeable players who ultimately serve the needs of the state. As an example, Serge Ménard defended Gosset at his criminal trial in 1988; in 1994 he was appointed Quebec's Public Security Minister (a position he no longer holds). He once defended Gosset's conduct and was later responsible for overseeing police practices. After his appointment, Ménard openly stated that there was no need for an independent civilian review board to oversee police abuses because of the lack of incidents. "It wouldn't be busy enough."[47]

When police officers are brought to trial, a conflict of interest exists because judges and prosecutors must distance themselves from police officers who usually work with the courts. Judge Trotier's mis-instruction to the jury and prosecutor Trudel's lack of initiative to adequately prosecute Gosset at his second trial are both illustrative of this. Judge Trotier increased the Crown's burden to prove a criminal state of mind when establishing Gosset's reckless use of a firearm would have sufficed. Prosecutor Trudel, at Gosset's second trial, did not focus on Gosset's reckless use of a firearm, but concentrated on establishing that Gosset's firearm was not inoperative. This strategy was tangential because the essential question was whether or not Gosset had been negligent in taking out his weapon—rather than whether his firearm malfunctioned. This approach resulted in Gosset's second acquittal and Trudel's statement that he felt justice had been served. Prosecutors prosecuting a police officer may find themselves unwilling to

Prosecutors prosecuting a police officer may find themselves unwilling to try the officer to the fullest extent of the law because, under normal circumstances, prosecutors rely on police officers to produce evidence which aids them in successfully prosecuting their cases. Normally, police officers are their allies and fellow workers, not their adversaries. This problem was tacitly acknowledged during the high profile Richard Barnabé case when an outside prosecutor was assigned to work with the Sûreté du Québec because MUC officers were being investigated. Claude Parent, the chief prosecutor for the Montreal region, stated that, because Montreal prosecutors often worked closely with many of the officers, impartiality would be questioned.

MUC POLICING INSTITUTION

There was an obvious internal struggle between the MUC administration, police chiefs, and the police brotherhood—the police union, which emerged as a result of the Gosset case. This struggle was crucial to the development and outcome of the various proceedings. Prior to the Anthony Griffin killing there had been on-going allegations of police harassment and brutality by members of the black community in Montreal. To many members of the black community the shooting of Anthony Griffin was a blatant example of the brutality that was symptomatic of the racism present within the MUC policing institution. The black community maintained that Gosset's unholstering of his firearm in the situation epitomized the distrust and brutality police officers exhibited towards blacks. Because of the black community's public outrage and unrelenting pressure immediately following the incident, Chief Bourget was obliged to act to avoid a community revolt. From the beginning Chief Bourget focused on the bad apple analogy, with Gosset singled out as a wrong-doer, to silence the black community's complaints about harassment and brutality. According to Bourget, Gosset's conduct was exceptional and contrary to acceptable police conduct. He denied that the incident was racially motivated and avoided acknowledging any police force accountability. By focusing attention on Gosset's individual misconduct Bourget attempted to direct attention away from the black community's claim that the MUC policing organization as a whole was, and is, racist. The Quebec Police Commission and the MUC concluded that Gosset's behaviour was unacceptable while denying that the incident was racially motivated.

The chief's decision to fire Gosset angered the police brotherhood, which openly accused their chief of scapegoating one of his officers to appease the black community. This allegation was partially correct. Chief Bourget did focus his energy on Gosset's conduct to appease the black community's charges of racism, while denying any overall responsibility. The brotherhood solidly supported Gosset throughout the proceedings and claimed that inadequate training and inoperative firearms caused the fatal incident— not racism. They were unwilling to expose any racist tendencies with the policing institution because the brotherhood would be implicated. This support, including the token cheque to Gosset from the brotherhood, is an indication that fellow officers supported Gosset's behaviour. Their support contradicted the chief's assertion that Gosset was one bad apple among many good apples. By accepting his conduct, the members of the brotherhood acknowledged that it was not a marked departure from how they would have acted under similar circumstances. The police brotherhood considered Gosset to be a victim who was taking the fall for the organization's technical inadequacies.

As the internal struggle between the chief and the brotherhood developed it became clear that the power base was with the brotherhood. Of a 45,000 member force, only 30 commanding officers were not union members. They overturned the chief's decision to dismiss Gosset by presenting their case to an outside labour arbitrator who ruled in their favour. Because of internal pressures the chief was powerless to discipline Gosset. The police brotherhood succeeded in reinstating Gosset, and Bourget resigned in November 1988. Bourget's replacement as chief, St. Germain, felt immediate pressure from the black community to appeal the arbitrator's decision of reinstatement. He also chose to rely on the bad apple theory to counter on-going allegations of racism and lack of police accountability. As a result, he faced similar internal opposition. The appeal to the arbitrator was denied. St. Germain accepted the brotherhood's demands regarding Gosset's early retirement to regain the support and respect of his officers.

After the incident St. Germain admitted to losing control over his men on several occasions because of the power of the police brotherhood. On

July 8, 1993, contrary to his express orders, the MUC police brotherhood halted patrols for seven hours and only responded to emergency calls in reaction to the threat of a salary freeze. St. Germain's efforts to prevent the work stoppage were ineffective. His press release stated:

> From 12:30 or 1 p.m. I realized very clearly that as chief of police I no longer had any control of public security on the territory of the MUC. All the responsibility, all the work of public security had been taken from me and was now in the hands of the president of the Brotherhood. All I could do was watch what was happening, hoping there wasn't going to be a tragedy on the territory of the MUC.[48]

There were other incidents following the Griffin shooting which demonstrated the power of the police brotherhood. It organized a 2000 officer demonstration because St. Germain accused the officers involved in the shooting death of Marcellus François of unjustifiable error.[49] On May 14, 1996 it was revealed that reports written about the Martin Suazo shooting by officers present at the shooting were submitted to the brotherhood before being given to Sûreté du Québec investigators. The brotherhood was thus able to rectify any inconsistencies in the statements before the investigators became involved. This was revealed at the Suazo inquest when an officer who had been holding one of Suazo's arms when Suazo was shot in the head testified that he received a call from the brotherhood requesting a statement.[50] The lawyer representing the Suazo family accused the brotherhood of running the police department. Sûreté du Québec investigators have worked with the MUC police brotherhood when investigating killings in the past. After the 1989 killing of Yvon Lafrance, ex-Sûreté investigator Gaetan Rivest recently admitted that the brotherhood coached the officers involved to coordinate their stories to avoid criminal prosecution.[51] It is indisputable that the brotherhood has a great deal of power within the police department and that it influences the attitudes of the MUC officers.

The End Result

Aside from the issue of racism which was consistently denied in every proceeding, after seven years of court cases and tribunals Allan Gosset was able to avoid accountability for the death of Anthony Griffin. At the outset he was charged with the reckless use of a firearm, which is punishable by a maximum two year prison term. The MUC policing institution agreed to grant Gosset's request for early retirement after 18 years of service. He is currently receiving 80 percent of his salary because of the mental anguish which he alleged left him unfit for duty. Other blue collar workers must serve at least 25 years before they receive such generous benefits. Prior to his retirement he was given a technical promotion into the specialized wiretapping and surveillance unit. Gloria Augustus was awarded $14,000 for compensation in her son's death, an amount insufficient to cover her legal fees.

Although the MUC police force maintains that the Gosset case has been a catalyst for reorganization, only two minor changes have been implemented. First, the MUC police force was equipped with newer and safer double-action firearms, even though the proceedings established that Gosset's single-action revolver was not inoperative. On May 31, 1995 Martin Suazo, a 23 year old Peruvian man, was shot in the back of the head by a double-action MUC revolver as he was lying on the ground waiting to be handcuffed. The officer involved also stated that his firearm went off accidentally, even though it was the new and improved double-action type. Second, as a result of the Gosset case, all deaths which occur while the victims were in MUC police custody are investigated by an outside police force, generally the Sûreté du Québec, rather than internally. But the police are still policing the police. Cases which followed Gosset's have clearly demonstrated that an investigation by the Sûreté du Québec is a feeble attempt by the policing institution to counter allegations of a lack of police accountability. Since the Gosset case Sûreté investigations have not resulted in any criminal trials. The result remains the same, police officers are not held accountable when they kill, regardless of the circumstances. Between 1987 and 1993, in both Montreal and Toronto, all of the officers involved in killings have been exonerated of criminal charges and have faced only token disciplinary action.

CHAPTER SIX

Government Response:
Window-dressing the Controversy

The issue of the use of excessive and deadly force by police has become an increasing concern for the police, government officials, the public at large, and in particular, visible minorities. Individual officers, as well as police organizations as a whole, are under increased scrutiny—especially by those interest groups which are most affected by their actions. Between 1987 and 1993 a number of organizational changes, mostly in Ontario, have been implemented by governments attempting to contain and control the on-going controversy. These organizational changes have increased the level of friction between both the police and the public and the police and the government. The debate has focused on the issues of race and whether or not the police and policing organizations are systemically racist.

The authority to legislate the police and policing rests with the provinces, and each province's legislation defines the structures and procedures for their police forces. This results in clear organizational differences between the provinces. The organizational changes in Ontario and Quebec are discussed below.

<u>ONTARIO</u>

Between 1987 and 1993 there were eleven incidents involving the use of deadly force by Toronto area police. Between 1989 and 1993 eight blacks were shot by the Metro Toronto and Peel Police Services.[1] Conflicting attitudes exist: the provincial government, the police, and the public disagree about whether or not racism played a role in these incidents.

In 1992 then premier Bob Rae commissioned Stephen Lewis to investigate race relations in Ontario after the shooting death of Raymond Lawrence provoked black and white youth groups into rioting in downtown Toronto.[2] The Lewis Report was based on a one-month project during which police officers, police officials, government officials, members of the general public, and the black community in particular were interviewed about current policing problems. The report concentrated on the Metro Toronto Police Service because most of the controversy has centred around this force's conduct. Lewis concluded that if racism did exist within the police organization, it was fundamentally anti-black racism because much of the police violence was directed against members of the black community. Although government officials acknowledged that there was a problem with the disproportionate number of incidents of excessive force involving blacks, there was no acknowledgement that it could be attributed to systemic racism within the police force. To date, in cases involving police shootings of black citizens, no commission has found direct evidence of a racist motivation. But many commission reports have indirectly acknowledged racism—with recommendations for better police-race relations, as well as for education in this area. Bob Rae affirmed that he believes that racism is inherent in Canadian society, and that it is thus not surprising that it exists within the police services. The policing agencies consider that their actions were being unnecessarily scrutinized because the right to use force is at the core of the police mandate. A Metro Toronto officer expressed his concern, "Unquestionably, every police officer feels hurt and anger by the way in which our integrity has come into question by some special interest groups, politicians and the media."[3]

Individual police officers genrally perceive themselves as being part of a cohesive unit where individual members support each other. When killing incidents occur the officer in question is generally welcomed back into the force with open arms by his or her peers. Typical is the David Denivey case, where criminal charges against officer Denivey for the shooting death of Lester Donaldson in Toronto provoked a police protest.[4] Police chiefs also support their officers, while at the same time acknowledging a need for improved training programs in both race relations and the use of firearms.[5] The policing institution assumes an adversarial position when accused of racism. Many officers believe that the force used when dealing with visible minorities is justified because of what they consider are clear patterns of criminality manifested by the black community.[6] Metro Toronto auditor Allan Andrews commented, "Almost universally, at all levels, we were told by officers that, even though there were no statistics to back it up, they knew who was committing the crimes and in many cases they were minorities."[7]

Ontario's black community is outraged by the increase in black deaths caused by police. Protests have been organized by blacks to voice their dissatisfaction, anger, and fear of the police. They believe that the police are racist and that racism affects how officers treat minority groups in the commission of their duties. The unpredictability of the police response in encounters with black youth has many families frightened. Wilson Head, past president of the Urban Alliance on Race Relations, said that it "looked like open season on black youths."[8]

In response, the Ontario government has implemented three important organizational changes concerning police use of force: the Special Investigations Unit (external review board), the Ontario Police Complaints Commission, and the Use of Force Report.

Criminal investigation into police conduct involving the use of deadly force is one of the most controversial issues within the criminal justice system. An external investigative body, the Special Investigations Unit (SIU), was created under Ontario's new *Police Services Act* in December 1990 in response to the increasing controversy around police shootings of blacks in Toronto during the 1980s. Prior to this act, Ontario police forces investigated officer wrong-doing internally, with the Ontario Provincial police investigating incidents involving officers from the Metro Toronto police and vice versa. This procedure was changed because of public accusations that the police were not impartial when investigating fellow officers. The SIU, which has all the investigative powers of the police, was created to review all matters involving death or serious injury caused by the police where the possibility of criminal charges exist. It is composed of 11 investigators, including two non-police staff and nine ex-police officers.[9]

Along with the formation of the SIU, the new law requires police services to hire more visible minorities and to set up civilian panels to consider complaints of police misconduct. The Solicitor-General stated that the SIU would "pave the way for policing in the 1990s."[10] Premier Bob Rae confirmed that an external investigative body is necessary to discipline officers who engage in wrong-doing. But the SIU has been plagued with long delays and a back-log of cases. Government officials are aware of valid police concerns over the delays by the Special Investigations Unit, but they do not agree that the unit has been inefficient, insisting that the main problem with the unit is its lack of investigators. Howard Morton, who once headed the unit, petitioned the government to increase the number of investigators to solve the delay problems.

Police departments do not support the Special Investigations Unit for a number of reasons. Officers feel that their actions are being unnecessarily questioned and that they are being unfairly singled out.[11] The principal complaint is that the SIU takes too long to investigate cases; the Ottawa Police Association president argues that the long delays in the investigations could endanger officers' lives. "It's an unnecessary stress, having this long investigation over your head. It could cause the officer to start second-guessing his own judgement... and that could cost the officer his life if he's in a dangerous situation."[12] Apart from problems involving delays, police also argue that Section 113 of the *Police Services Act*, which states "that officers must cooperate fully with SIU members conducting investigations" infringes on Section 11(C) of the *Canadian Charter of Rights and Freedoms*; "Any person charged with an offence has the right not to be compelled to be a witness in proceedings against that person in respect of the offence."[13] Officers have refused to cooperate with the SIU, stating that it infringes on their constitutional rights; that being compelled to take part in an SIU investigation, when the possibility of criminal charges being laid against them exists, violates their Charter rights. The Attorney-General has stipulated that any officer who refuses to take part in an SIU investigation would be breaking the law because the "prevailing view is that the public's right to hold Police accountable overrides any Constitutional issue (which could be raised by police)."[14] Police officers believe that internal investigations by the provincial police force should continue. Their rejection of the SIU has met with open opposition. In Toronto police have invoked their right to run a parallel internal investigation under terms of an agreement made with the province.[15]

Visible minority communities lack confidence in the SIU because they do not believe that the use of ex-police officers to investigate police misconduct will result in fair and impartial findings. They believe that people with non-police backgrounds should be trained to investigate such matters. The government disagrees, considering that the investigators need to be sensitive to, and knowledgeable about, the police culture.[16] Although black community leaders agree that the SIU needs changes, including a greater reliance on non-police personnel, they believe that the unit should not be dismantled. They urge members of the black community to press the government to allocate the resources necessary to permit the SIU to carry out its investigations in a timely and efficient manner. One leader stated that "Police power is legitimate, real and, when enforced, could have very serious consequences on the public at large. This power *cannot* go unchecked, and the police, like other public servants, must be held accountable for their actions."[17]

After the Special Investigations Unit has investigated an incident, its report, which includes a recommendation about whether or not criminal charges should be laid against the officer(s) involved, is presented to the chief. The report is then transferred to the Ontario Police Complaints Commission, a branch of the Attorney General's Office, which deals with public complaints of police misconduct. A civilian complaint can also be made directly with the Office of the Police Complaints Commissioner or at any police detachment.[18] The Complaints Commission was created as a civilian review agency with a mandate to recommend changes to police policy and to call for disciplinary boards of inquiry. It cannot resolve a complaint directly; but it is empowered to issue a report detailing the facts of the case to the chief of the police service involved. It is the police chief and/or the Police Services Board which then decides what action should be taken. This decision, which must be made within six months of a completed investigation, may be to verbally reprimand the officer, hold a disciplinary hearing, ask the Complaints Commission to hold a public hearing, lay criminal charges, or take no further action.[19] Although individual officers might be reprimanded based on the Committee's recommendations, the response has rarely involved policy changes. If the complainant, either the victim or the victim's family, does not agree with the chief's decision, there are thirty days to request a review. It is at this point that the Complaints Commission decides whether or not the case should be sent to the board of inquiry.[20] Officers charged or suspended pending a hearing are not suspended without pay unless they have been convicted of a criminal offence.

The Attorney General's office has stated that most of the criticism of the Ontario Police Complaints Commission are a result of its limited powers. Although its main task is to settle disputes between the police and the public, the Complaints Commission has neither the power nor the authority to discipline the police. In approximately 95 percent of the cases which the office has investigated, the police chief involved later dropped the complaint. The process is too long and complicated to be effective but the present structure is necessary because of the need for a sharing of power between the police and a complaints office.[21]

One lawyer in the 1980's who pressed for a civilian body to investigate police misconduct, argued that the Complaints Commission should be dismantled because the existing structure makes it more difficult to lodge a successful citizen's complaint against the police. "The chances of getting a cop disciplined are about one in a hundred, I would say. ...It's the illusion of accountability."[22] Edwart Walters, editor of *Spectrum*, a visible minority newspaper, also believes that the time lag renders the Complaints Commission ineffective. Complainants are left with nothing but costly lawyers' fees.

In response to the recommendations of the Lewis Report, the use of the Use of Force Report[23] was implemented in February, 1993 (See Appendix 3). Ontario officers are required to complete this report every time they draw or use their firearms in public. The Ontario Ministry of the Solicitor General has confirmed that the data will be used to produce yearly statistical information about the types and frequency of force used by police. No data had previously been compiled which could determine whether or not police officers were using force in an acceptable manner. This information would then be used to help redefine policy and devise new training initiatives for the use of force. Studies based on the use of force data are conducted annually and are not intended to identify individual officers, but to provide information concerning the amount and type of force used by police officers overall. The Ontario *Police Services Act* confirms the requirement for use of the Use of Force report. Each member of the police force is obliged to submit a report to the chief of police or Commissioner whenever that member (a) draws a handgun in the presence of a member of the public, excluding a member of the police force while on duty, or discharges a firearm; (b) uses a weapon other than a firearm on another person; or (c) uses physical force on another person that results in an injury requiring medical attention.[24] The section does not apply when the handgun is drawn during training. Section B of the report, which contains all the personal information about the officer involved, is destroyed no later than thirty days after it is submitted. It may be retained for an additional period, not exceeding two years, if the board deems it necessary for a determination of whether or not the officer should receive additional training. The report cannot be used to implicate any officer of any wrong-doing or be submitted into evidence at any internal disciplinary hearing or Police Complaints Commission hearing as defined under the *Police Services Act*. Police service boards can, however, authorize a review of the report by other supervisory levels or review committees.[25]

Police officers generally have not acknowledged any need for the Use of Force Report,[26] and are concerned that reports could be used retro-actively if criminal proceedings were to be brought against an officer. The belief exists that the report could cause officers to hesitate about whether or not to draw their guns and place them at greater risk. The obligation to complete the report aligned them against the New Democratic Party government which passed the legislation. The Police Association president of Metro Toronto blamed politicians for interfering and pitting the public against the police.[27] Officers demonstrated their disapproval of the Use of Force Report in 1993 by refusing to wear their uniform caps, badges, and identification numbers and by reducing the number of speeding and illegal parking tickets they issued.[28]

QUEBEC

As in Toronto, Montreal policing has come under increasing public scrutiny arising from allegations of brutality and the abuse of power. Based on numerous questionable police killings, blacks and other visible minority groups have accused the MUC police of racism. Between 1987 and 1993 the Montreal Urban Community police force killed ten individuals; five blacks, three hispanics and two whites. When confronted, the Quebec government and policing officials have done less than their Ontario counterparts to implement organizational changes. The province's only action to date has been the implementation of campaigns promoting the hiring of visible minorities into the police forces and the creation of the Quebec Police Ethics Commission. Although there have been discussions about using special civilian investigative units to investigate all police shootings, none have yet been implemented.

There have been numerous reports on police and race relations resulting from these questionable police shootings. Most notable is the 1988 Bellemaire report, a major police-minority relations report from a task force headed by Jacques Bellemaire, who also headed the Quebec Human Rights Commission.[29] The task force was formed to examine relations between the police and visible minorities after the killing of Anthony Griffin in 1987. A key recommendation in the report was that significant effort should be made to establish equal opportunity hiring on Quebec police forces to achieve a more culturally representative police service. More specifically, the report recommended that police forces in Quebec should have a ten percent visible minority component by 1995.

The recent controversies have pushed the Nicolet Police Academy to institute a two-day training course on interculturalism designed to sensitize officers to the cultural differences of the many groups living in Quebec. The institute's former Director of Pedagogical Services stated that he believed that many of the recent police problems could be attributed to officers not understanding these cultural differences, rather than to chronic racism within the forces.[30]

Police officers have expressed resentment about the criticism which they have received recently over the number of shootings and the allegation that racism has played a role in the shootings. They have argued that their firearms are their only protection, and that the decision to use them is a split-second one, implying that shooting deaths by police officers are a given. These split-second decisions, according to one constable, are very wearing on the officers; "It takes nerves of steel. As a police officer… our service revolver is all we have."[31]

There has been growing concern in the black community about blacks being the primary group being killed by Montreal police. This has caused open questioning of police conduct about the use of excessive force. Dan Philip, president of the Black Coalition of Quebec, commented on the shooting of Trevor Kelly in 1993 in Montreal, "Whenever the police approach people in our community, their guns are always drawn and pointing at us. ...Our community has found, time and time again, that the conduct of the Police is unacceptable....[w]e don't want police to be judge, jury and executioners of our young people."[32] Noel Alexander, president of the Jamaican Association in Montreal, believes that the police are much more aggressive with the non-white community. He declared that if this hostile behaviour did not stop, visible minorities would eventually retaliate. He said, "Once they see a person who's a shade darker than they are, whether the person is black or of a different ethnic group, police behave in an aggressive manner." [33] The director of the Bureau of the Haitian Christian Community of Montreal also shares the conviction that uncontrollable violence will eventually erupt between the police and the black community if conditions do not change.[34]

Two important subjects, the lack of an external investigative body, and the usefulness of the coroner's inquest, must be addressed. Under the current Quebec system, the Quebec Provincial Police (Sûreté du Québec) investigates incidents of deadly force committed by the MUC, and the MUC investigates incidents involving deadly force committed by the provincial police. Once an investigation is completed a report is forwarded to both the Public Security Minister and the crown prosecutor's office— where a joint decision is reached about whether or not criminal charges should be laid. All shootings which do not result in death are investigated internally by the force involved. Because there are no non-police investigators, serious questions about whether or not investigations can be unbiased exist. There have been many accusations of lack of impartiality.

Former Quebec Public Security Minister Claude Ryan considered whether or not Quebec should follow Ontario's lead and create an external review board to investigate police shootings. This was in response to coroner Harvey Yarosky's report into the fatal shooting of Marcellus François in

1991. Yarosky stated that a thorough review of the use of force tactics by the MUC police in the killing should have been conducted; and that, in the future, police-instigated shootings should be investigated externally.[35] He maintained that a review was needed because of the MUC police service's blatantly racist conduct in the François incident. Ryan agreed that a review of police practices should be conducted and called upon Albert Malouf, a retired Quebec Court of Appeal judge, to conduct the review. Malouf's conclusion was that there was a need for a civilian-led external review board. He also advised the Public Security Minister to call a public debate to allow the various communities to voice their concerns and request specific guidelines to curb existing MUC police misconduct.[36] Former MUC police chief Alain St. Germain did not believe that such a review was necessary because he did not believe that the force was racist. He accused Yarosky and his report of discrediting the entire force over one specific incident. Another coroner, Teresa Sourour, who investigated the death of Trevor Kelly, also made recommendations to Ryan concerning the need for a civilian investigative unit.[37] She stated that an internal review alone "could cloud the appearance of justice" and that, "a special investigative unit would allow police officers to avoid the paradoxical situation where they are called upon to investigate an act committed by one of their own."[38] Despite the two coroners' recommendations, Claude Ryan concluded that there was no immediate need for changes because he had faith in the police to adequately investigate shootings by fellow officers.[39]

Leaders of the black community have consistently expressed their dissatisfaction with the current system of internal investigative bodies.[40] Dan Philip, after reading coroner Teresa Sourour's report, agreed that a civilian body should be set up to investigate police shootings. He said, "[r]ight now, the MUC and the SQ don't really investigate each other's shootings. They just corroborate each other's versions."[41]

The black community's charge of corruption in the current system of investigations was validated on May 16, 1996, when an ex-Sûreté du Québec investigator, Gaetan Rivest, admitted in a *Gazette* article about police corruption that he and fellow officers had fabricated evidence to cover up all killings caused by the MUC police.[42] Rivest used the investigation into the death of Yvon Lafrance in 1989, which he took part in, as an example of such fabrications. The investigation concluded that the shooting was justified because the officer's life was in danger. At a press conference Rivest produced his written statement which demonstrated how the Sûrété du Québec falsified evidence to protect an officer from criminal prosecution. He revealed that during the investigation the officer admitted to him that his life was not in danger but that he shot Lafrance out of nervousness. Lafrance did not lunge towards the officer with a knife, as the investigation concluded, but was moving away from the officer when shot. Rivest and other investigators coached the officers who had been at the scene to provide similar accounts of how Lafrance had lunged forward. Rivest also related how the crime-scene technicians helped set up the scene to correspond with the MUC officers' statements. Lafrance, armed with a knife, was placed four to ten feet away from the officer, rather than the 15 to 25 feet which was actually the case. "Arranging the crime scenes was just like making a movie," Rivest reminisced. Mock courts were set up where witnesses were questioned in order to gauge whether or not their responses would corroborate with the official police version of events. When asked why he covered up for the MUC, Rivest answered, "As far as I was concerned, we were all police officers and we protected each other."[43]

The second issue which emerged around the questionable killings by the MUC police concerns the usefulness of a coroner's inquest. A coroner's inquest is held to investigate the circumstances surrounding the death of a civilian while in police custody. The resulting report's purpose is to inform the public about the circumstances of the incident and outline recommendations arising from an analysis of the incident to avoid a recurrence of a similar situation in the future.[44] Although Quebec coroners were once given the responsibility of determining whether or not criminal charges should be laid against an officer involved in a shooting, after 1986 they were no longer empowered to do so.[45] Without this power coroners now make non-binding recommendations. The two coroner's reports mentioned above each called for a civilian review board to investigate shootings, but the Public Security Minister did not implement that recommendation. The usefulness of the inquest is questionable. Many community leaders have expressed their dissatisfaction with the impotence of the coroner's inquest and report, which are understood to be attempts to appease interest groups and contribute to the illusion that something is being done. Dan Philip concurred, stating that coroner's inquests are useless because, although they outline the circumstances of the case, they have no real power or authority to lay charges.[46]

Between 1987 and 1993 Quebec has implemented only one organizational change with regard to the police and the use of force—the Quebec Police Ethics Committee. The Committee is an administrative tribunal created in September 1990 to deal specifically with public complaints against police misconduct.[47] It is composed of lawyers, police officers appointed by the police chief, and civilians appointed by the Montreal municipal government. The committee adheres to the Quebec Code of Police Ethics, which includes a 14-section set of rules defining police norms of conduct in their dealings with the public sector. Section 6 of the code focuses directly on the police abuse of authority (See Appendix 4).[48]

The Police Ethics Committee deals with initial complaints as well as appeals to decisions reached by the committee. If the committee concludes that an officer has breached the code, the decision about the course of action to be taken is made by a three-member panel consisting of a lawyer, a police officer and a civilian. There are five possible sanctions which may be imposed on an officer who is found to have contravened the code of ethics: a warning, a reprimand, a suspension not exceeding 60 days, a demotion or job termination.[49] The committee is not mandated to impose criminal sanctions. The appeal of a prior decision to the committee is the last step in the complaints process; thus once a decision has been reached, it is final.

The committee also publishes an annual report which is submitted to the Public Security Minister, containing statistics on its yearly caseload. Fifty percent of the total complaints made against the police in Quebec in 1993 involved the abuse of force. Specifically, 55 percent of those abuse cases involved contravention of Section 6 of the Code of Ethics, abuse of authority, which forbids officers from resorting to use of greater force than necessary; using threats, intimidation or harassment; charging someone without justification; abusing authority to obtain a statement; and detaining in order to question a person who is not under arrest. The use of a firearm without justification in Section 11 of the Code accounted for the remaining four percent of abuse of force complaints.[50]

The committee, which in 1993 had a $2.5 million budget, reviewed a total of 121 complaints, and concluded that only 28 merited sanctions. Of the 80 appeals entered, 70 were rejected. There were a total of 21 disciplinary sanctions enforced—four warnings, two reprimands, 14 suspensions of one-to-ten days, and one job termination.[51] The job termination resulted from an incident in 1990 during which an officer arrested a strip-club dancer after she refused his sexual advances. The officer involved was charged with making false accusations, conflict of interest and illegal arrest.[52]

Little effort has been made by the Quebec government and policing officials to legislate changes to monitor and control police abuses of authority. The Police Ethics Commission is inadequate to process and address citizen complaints. Although it purports to be an impartial police review agency, it is comprised of official state agents, police officers, lawyers, and government appointed civilians. Input by communities and interest groups most affected by police abuses is non-existent; the commission cannot represent and address the general public's concerns. The police are still policing themselves.

The only other suggestion by the Quebec government was for increased minority hiring. The goal of a ten percent visible minority presence on the MUC force by 1995 has not been met. In 1994 the MUC force had 4337 officers, only 38 of whom were visible minorities— less than one percent of the total force. The MUC policing institution continues to maintain that members of visible minority groups, especially from the black community, do not apply to join the police force. However, between April 1993 and April 1994, of 1171 individuals who applied and were eligible to become MUC police officers, 128 were visible minorities, or 10.9 percent of applicants. This failure cannot be attributed to the lack of visible minority applicants,[53] but rather to a lack of initiative by the policing institution to hire visible minorities.

Although it would appear that Ontario has done more to address the issue of police abuse of force, the essential problem has not changed. The organizational changes have been an exercise in window dressing. The SIU has not improved the reality of the lack of impartiality in the investigation of officer wrong-doing. The backlog of cases causes excessive delays which renders it ineffective in disciplining officers. Due to the contradictory nature of its mandate, the SIU is powerless to compel officers to cooperate with investigators, preventing any comprehensive investigations. Most importantly, as discussed by leaders of the black community, the choice of ex-police officers to head the investigations jeopardizes impartiality. The purpose of such a unit was to address allegations that police internal review board members were sympathetic to officers under review. Staffing the SIU with ex-police officers prejudiced it from the outset. The review agency which deals specifically with public complaints, the Police Complaints Commission, is powerless because it can only recommend disciplinary action and policy changes. Many of the recommendations have not been accepted by the Metro police chief, who makes the final decision.

The *Use of Force* report was another attempt by the Ontario government to silence public outrage. The negative police reaction to using the report created the impression that it was a major initiative. On a practical level the report is ineffective. Once a report is completed by the officer and reviewed by a supervisor the only required action is a recommendation for additional training. Focusing narrowly on training undermines community demands for officer accountability. Since the report cannot be used at police disciplinary hearings, it cannot implicate individual officers in wrong-doing, nor does it serve as a deterrent.

One can conclude from the recent debates that the institutional changes implemented have done little to address community concerns. The changes have not reduced the number of incidents of police abuse of force in either province. When shooting incidents occur, there are public calls for police accountability. Government and policing institution responses have been to transform the problem into a need for increased training and institutionalized policy changes. Government action remains at the level of citizen appeasement—with little attempt to curb the problem. The issue of race and racism is consistently denied and remains unaddressed.

State and policing organizations are unwilling to implement concrete change to reduce current problems. The history of policing demonstrates that, from the beginning, policing organizations have not been neutral. Policing organizations were designed to promote and protect the interests of those in power with military styled policing organizations. There is little reason to assume that our current policing institutions are more impartial or neutral than they were at their inception.

Although policing institutions present themselves as serving all members of society equally, some groups in society are more equally served than others. To acknowledge the police brutality problem, especially against visible minority groups, would require that policing organizations accept responsibility for the actions of their officers. This acknowledgement would put into question the legitimacy of the use of physical force. Since the use of force is at the essence of the police mandate, questioning its inappropriate use would involve questioning the entire structure which trained its officers. If the policing structure is, by definition, flawed, the state from which it has emerged must bear some responsibility. Focusing attention on the inherent problems of policing institutions would cause the premise of fair and equal treatment for all to be proved invalid. The state cannot be relied on to initiate effective changes within the policing organization alone; other citizen-initiated avenues must also be explored.

CHAPTER SEVEN

Where Do We Go from Here?

A woman is walking by the riverside when she sees a body floating downstream. A nearby fisherman jumps into the water, pulls out the drowning man and saves his life. Moments later, another drowning body is seen floating downstream, and once again the fisherman rescues the person only to see another body in the water in the need of assistance. This cycle continues until finally the fisherman ignores the next body floating by and instead begins to walk upstream. The woman asks him, "What are you doing? Why aren't you saving that drowning man as you have been?" The fisherman replies, "I'm going upstream to find out what or who is throwing them into the water in the first place." [1]

The previous chapter discussed the futility of focusing on police policy to address police misconduct and excessive use of force. Since the action taken by governments and police organizations relates to policy when dealing with police excesses, it is citizens who must determine what should be done. One effective action would be to dismantle the whole structure.

Because the police problem is based on its exclusive power base, any change would require a redefinition of that power. Police officers have the right to use physical force with the assurance of no real public accountability. Dismantling the police institution is the only option that would guarantee an end to the current wave of unjustified killings and other police abuses of power But it is not possible. Dismantling the police would require a re-conceptualization and re-definition of our entire society.

The value and trust that society confers on its policing institutions, coupled with the fear of rampant crime, would make dismantling impossible. The presence of a policing organization is considered natural. Societies accept the need for centralized governments and controlling bodies to function properly. We assume that without the coercive aspect of present-day policing, disorder and chaos would prevail. When individual police officers abuse their power it is the particular action itself which is questioned, not the existence of the institution as a whole. It is difficult to convince the general public of the need for such questioning.

The flaws within the policing institution must be viewed within the context of the system's conception of crime and justice. The capitalist nature of western societies causes, de facto, crime and justice to be defined in a manner which accommodates an economic structure based on the accumulation of private property. One feature of capitalism is greed, the desire to accumulate individual wealth and property. Capitalism promotes a survival of the fittest mentality rather than the concept of the good of the whole.

Definitions of crime are not an absolute because, as has been demon-strated throughout history, what has been considered a crime has changed to accommodate the needs of society. Our society engenders inequality, so a control mechanism, the police, is needed to ensure its survivial. When the idea of crime comes to mind, most people envision one person attacking another on a street—and the attacker is not wearing a suit and tie. Few people imagine a company executive behind a desk cutting back on safety measures to increase profits. The company executives responsible for the deaths of 14 miners at Westray due to unsafe conditions are not considered mass murderers. We do not indict government officials for not enforcing safety regulations. The police focus their efforts on property and street crimes in an attempt to control and pacify the people at the bottom of the economic ladder. These individuals are more likely to enter the criminal justice system. White collar crimes are considered somehow less criminal. Even when the wealthy commit crimes considered the domain of the lower classes, they are more likely to be exonerated because our legal system is one law for the rich and one for the poor. Those who can afford the best legal counsel are more likely to be acquitted.

Since the concept of crime is malleable, the conception of justice is also blurred. Justice, in the context of capitalism, cannot be achieved because fairness and equality are philosophical concepts. The interests of some are sacrificed for the benefit of others.

Dismantling policing organizations and replacing them with alternative structures would result in the creation of new police-style structures with similar problems.[2] This cannot be achieved within our current society. There are less radical and more practical options available. We must realize that any action other than the elimination of the police is a piecemeal solution. The choice is between doing nothing and doing something. Perhaps, by taking action on a small scale, over time meaningful change will occur.

The most viable alternative is citizen-initiated opposition to expose on-going abuses. Citizen groups should avoid the goal of organizational policy changes because engaging in policy debates does not produce results. Concerned groups become trapped in a bureaucratic web where legitimate concerns about police abuses are co-opted and redefined with no attempt being made to address the primary causes. The Citizens' Independent Review of Police Activities (CIRPA) in Toronto was caught in such a web. CIRPA, which was created to help complainants, failed because of state interference and eventual co-opting.

CIRPA emerged from a mass movement against police brutality in 1981 in Toronto, as a result of questionable police tactics, primarily the shooting death of Albert Johnson in 1979 by a Metro Toronto police officer, and a series of gay bathhouse raids in 1981. On August 26, 1979 Albert Johnson, a black immigrant from Jamaica was shot in his home by Toronto police officers. The police stated that they acted in self-defence after Johnson threatened them with a lawn edger. Johnson's daughter, who witnessed her father's death, maintained that he was shot while he was kneeling down. Johnson had previously complained to the Ontario Human Rights Commission about police harassment. Although two officers were charged with manslaughter, both were acquitted. On February 5, 1981 more than two hundred police officers raided four gay bathhouses and charged over 300 hundred people with indecency.[3] These events fuelled the momentum for a demand for greater controls on police powers, and led to the enactment of Bill 68—an *Act for Establishment and Conduct of a Project in the Municipality of Metropolitan Toronto to Improve Methods of Processing Complaints by Members of the Public Against Police Officers on the Metropolitan Police Force* (1981). Although this bill empowered the Police Complaints Board to impose disciplinary penalties, it also allowed the police to conduct initial investigations for thirty days. Community leaders lobbied to change the bill to stipulate that investigations would be conducted entirely by civilians. The Ontario government's rejection of this recommendation led to the creation of CIRPA.

CIRPA's initial goal was to establish itself as an unofficial alternative civilian complaints group at the grass-roots level to aid complainants in pursuing their cases.[4] CIRPA demanded a public meeting between its members and the police and openly opposed the Public Complaints Commissioner's Office, maintaining that it was useless. CIRPA attempted to gain recognition through the media and by bringing details of individual complaints to police commission meetings. It openly attacked the uselessness of the proposed civilian review and provoked an angry response from the police commission chairman. He accused CIRPA of "encouraging a system of espionage and sabotage on law enforcement officers who are sworn to uphold the law. What are these? Vigilante activities?"[5] CIRPA's position and activities at police commission meetings caused hostility. The police Commissioner's office passed a motion which disallowed public allegations of police brutality, undermining CIRPA's ability to carry out its mandate.

Frustrated, CIRPA compromised on its demand for a public meeting and agreed to meet police commission members in private. At this point CIRPA's original reform goals were co-opted into state controlled reforms, and meetings between the two organizations became friendly. By 1982 CIRPA had turned away from grass-roots involvement to administration and policy issues which were on the police commission's agenda. It joined the policing organization's discourse and began to focus on issues of professional expertise rather than aiding complainants. In response to six incidents of police abuse of force—the use of billyclubs to control large crowds—CIRPA recommended a review of police policies, guidelines and training, without dealing with specific allegations of brutality. This shift served the needs of the police commission and provided a rubber-stamp opposition. A police commission member stated, "[E]very organization needs not only a gadfly to keep them honest and to keep them thinking, but a horsefly, something that will come in and bite and hurt and draw blood from time to time. I think it's very valuable, it's part of the system…

I'm glad they're there."[6] Once under police control, the horsefly, CIRPA, was proof that opposition concerns were being addressed. But CIRPA was transformed from a grass-roots organization into a supporter of the police organization in its attempt to gain legitimacy. Eventually all of its decision-making was focused on legitimizing itself before the police commission rather than on aiding complainants.

There were two reasons for CIRPA's strategy change which led to being co-opted. The policing institution is, de facto, legitimate, and civilian organizations are not; CIRPA compromised to gain legitimacy. By aligning itself more closely with the police, it acquired credibility after sacrificing its original goal of dealing with individual complaints. Immediate legitimacy could only be achieved by compromising its established goals and adopting those of the policing institution. A citizen's group must remain in opposition and avoid engaging in the police institution's discourse.

CIRPA also failed to understand the extent of the police institution's ability to take over and transform it. Engaging with institutions to address concerns is dangerous because original mandates are often manipulated and redefined according to the institution's requirements.

Citizen's action groups must define goals based on four considerations:

1 Aiding complainants and/or their families

When incidents of police abuse occur, it is the victim and/or the family who requires support to pursue criminal prosecution and civil liability changes against the implicated officer and the policing institution, as well as ensuring that disciplinary action is taken. Any group working to address current abuses should be geared towards grass-roots initiatives which include aiding the victims.

2 Individual versus organizational accountability

In individual incidents of police abuses, citizen groups can choose to focus responsibility on either the police officer involved or the policing organization as a whole. When citizen groups attempt to do both they become involved in an overwhelming struggle which is self-defeating. Given the choice, opting for focusing on individual accountability is more effective for three reasons.

a) Calling for individual accountability initially promotes the bad apple theory of an implicated officer who has over-stepped the allowable guidelines of the policing mandate. But it is the organization which is ultimately responsible for the conduct of its officers, and attempting to implicate the entire police structure has, to date, resulted in policy changes which do not address the basic problems. Policing organizations have demonstrated, time and again, that they cannot be relied on to redefine exclusive powers, the catalyst for change must develop outside the existing power structures. Focusing on individual accountability does not prevent the questioning of the conduct of police institutions.

Support for officers involved in misconduct and a lack of will to discipline them are indicative of the belief that these incidents of abuse are trivial and do not require any modification. The names of police officers in Montreal are no longer released to the public until a decision to lay criminal charges is made. This was not so in the past. In the 1987 Anthony Griffin case Allan Gosset's name was released the day after the incident. In the Martin Suazo case in 1995 the officer's name was only revealed to the family and public several months after the killing, after the prosecution decided not to lay criminal charges. Although organizational accountability is the ultimate goal, successes in individual accountability, when coupled with the organization's unwillingness to reprimand, will stain the reputation of the entire policing organization.

b) Short term reforms geared towards individual accountability are well suited to achieving improvement within the police system. Goals built on short term reforms must be aimed at negating the basic premise of police legitimacy. Gearing efforts towards large-scale organizational accountability results in policy changes which strengthen the institutions.

3 Public safety

Public safety is the third element in any emphasis on individual officers' accountability. When officers abuse their power and use excessive force, how can we, as a society, feel or be safe when these same officers resume their duties? Many officers involved in unjustified abuses are still on the police force— even officers found criminally liable for their conduct while on duty. In the Richard Barnabé case in Montreal, Chief Duschesneau stated that the officers found guilty of aggravated assault for their part in the beating may be allowed to resume their duties after having served their prison sentences. The law stipulates that people applying to become police officers cannot have a criminal record, but the officers involved were already police officers when they were convicted.[7] A decision about these officers will be made once all disciplinary proceedings are concluded. Indicted officers who beat a man to death could eventually return to work as police officers.

4 Demanding information

A critical obstacle which contributes to camouflaging police abuse is the lack of information available to the public about how abusers are disciplined. When an incident occurs there is sporadic media coverage with little overall analysis or discussion. This often results in the loss of public interest and a misunderstanding of the situation.

Since the media cannot be relied on to pursue information, citizen groups should focus on this area. The information about investigations, disciplinary hearings, criminal and civil proceedings, public inquiries and coroner's inquests is not confidential. It is, however, protected by many bureaucratic layers, and almost inaccessible. Exposing action or inaction allows citizen groups to discover inadequacies and inconsistencies within the processes of investigations and decision-making. Continual demands for information would also reinforce the mandate of the watchdog group.

d) keeping issues in public eye

Any controversy presented in the media is only news while it is hot. Incidents of police abuse of power must remain in the public eye, or they are forgotten except by those who are personally affected by them.

Immediate meaningful change is impossible. The unwillingness of government, police and the community to redefine our society means that such change must be a long- term goal. Continually exposing police-inflicted injustice will gradually erode the legitimacy of policing organizations. Only then will we, as a society, begin to question its very existence. Until then, only on-going scrutiny will compel the police to conduct themselves with restraint.

Appendix One

Coverage of Police Violence
Montreal *Gazette*
June 1995

<u>THE GAZETTE ARTICLES (June 1995)</u>

	Richard Barnabé	Martin Suazo	SQ Tactics	Total # Articles
June 1:	---	---	1	1
June 2:	1	1	---	2
June 3:	1	1	---	2
June 4:	---	1	---	1
June 5:	1	---	1	2
June 6:	1	---	---	1
June 7:	1	---	---	1
June 8:	1	2	---	3
June 9:	2	---	---	3
June 10:	---	---	---	---
June 11:	---	1	---	1
June 12:	1	---	---	1
June 13:	1	---	---	1
June 14:	1	1	1	3
June 15:	1	---	---	1
June 16:	---	---	1	1
June 17:	1	3	1	5
June 18:	---	---	---	---
June 19:	---	---	2	2
June 20:	1	---	3	4
June 21:	1	1	2	4
June 22:	1	1	---	2
June 23:	1	---	1	2
June 24:	---	---	---	---
June 25:	---	---	---	---
June 26:	1	---	---	1
June 27:	7	---	1	8
June 28:	1	---	1	2
June 29:	3	---	1	4
June 30:	---	---	1	1
Total:	29	12	17	59

Victims of Police Use of Force 1993-1997

<u>MONTREAL</u>

Victim: **Richard Barnabé**
Race: White
Date: December 14, 1993
(See Chapter 3)

Victim: **Paolo Romanelli**
Race: White
Date: March 9, 1995
Shot and killed by police after he stabbed a police officer. The police had gone to his house because he had called 911 and said he needed to talk to an officer. When the police arrived, Romanelli allegedly lunged at one officer and stabbed him in the shoulder and barricaded himself in the house. The police broke into the house through the basement and shot him twice after he allegedly lunged at an officer with a kitchen knife. The victim's family sued the MUC because at the time of the crisis (when he barricaded himself in the house) the police would not allow his mother or father to speak to him in an attempt to calm him down.
(Montreal *Gazette*, March 11, 1995: A1, A8)

Victim: **Martin Suazo**
Race: Hispanic
Date: May 31, 1995
(See Chapter 3)

Victim: **Phillipe Ferraro**
Race: White
Date: June 26, 1995
(See Chapter 3)

Victim: **Nelson Herreault**

Race: Unknown

Date: April 15, 1996

He was arrested for failing to return to a halfway house. The police stated that they were forced to use pepper spray because he had resisted violently. In a holding cell at the police station Herreault began having convulsions. He was taken to a nearby hospital where he later died. The cause of death was deemed to be cocaine use even though combining pepper spray with the drug creates a lethal mix.

(*Globe & Mail*, April 17, 1996: pp. A8)

Victim: **Daniel Bélair**

Race: White

Date: May 17, 1996

Shot dead by MUC police on a Montreal street after an alleged armed robbery spree. He was shot several times after attempting to steal a woman's car at gunpoint. Bélair had escaped from a detoxification centre where he had been remanded by the court.

(Montreal *Gazette*, May 19, 1996: A1, A2)

Victim: **Michel Mathurin**

Race: White

Date: June 17, 1996

Mathurin, an unemployed janitor, was shot dead after allegedly threatening his ex-boss and two police officers with a pair of knives. He had been fired from his job the previous day.

(Montreal *Gazette*, June 18, 1996: A3)

Victim: **Unidentified**

Race: Unknown

Date: November 9, 1996

He was involved in a hit and run accident which ultimately led to crashing his car into a tree. Armed with a syringe, he sought refuge in a nearby apartment where he threatened the occupants. The police alleged that since he had violently resisted being arrested, they used pepper spray in order to handcuff him. He suffered a cariac arrest on the apartment floor and later died in hospital. The police alleged that the use of the pepper spray had no effect on him.

(Montreal *Gazette*, November 10, 1996: A3)

TORONTO

Victim: **Albert Moses**
Race: Black
Date: September 30, 1994
Moses, a mentally unstable man, was shot in the head by Constable Vance after he allegedly attacked a plainclothes officer with a hammer. The family urged the SIU to require the officers involved to turn over evidence (which they refused to do) and demanded to know why the police were at the rooming house where the incident occurred. The officers were cleared of any wrongdoing.

(*Toronto Star*, March 5, 1995: A6)

Victim: Albert Gale
Race: Unknown
Date: March 18, 1995
Died in hospital after collapsing in police custody after an alleged seizure He was arrested by police on theft charges.

(*Toronto Star*, November 13, 1995: A20)

Victim: **Osbaldo Aldama**
Race: Hispanic
Date: September 16, 1995
Police allege that he collapsed while in police custody because he had been using crack cocaine. He had been arrested by police for breaking and entering. A witness stated that she saw him on the floor lying on his stomach with his hands cuffed behind his back and that he was having difficulty breathing.

(*Toronto Star*, September 17, 1995: A7)

Victim: **Tony Viveiros**
Race: White
Date: November 11, 1995
Died in police custody after being arrested for a shooting incident. Viveiros' family insisted that the police were evasive in explaining what happened to their son and also stated that they were given different explanations as to what had occured. The police informed the family that he was having difficulty breathing and was therefore taken to the hospital, even though a police news release stated that he showed no sign of life back at the station. At the hospital, after a three hour wait during which the family was led to believe that he was having problems breathing, they were informed that he had died.

(*Toronto Star*, November 13, 1995:.A1, A20)

Victim: **Tommy Anthony Barnett**
Race: Black
Date: January 10, 1996
He was shot 4 times after allegedly threatening 2 officers with a sword. The issue that was investigated by the SIU was whether or not the police had fired a warning shot. His family described the shooting as 'wicked and unnecessary' while the police stated that it was self-defence. Family and friends of the victim accused the police of being racist against blacks. The officer involved was cleared of any wrong-doing by the SIU. At the inquest the judge refused to consider racism as an issue.

(*Toronto Star*, January 16, 1996: A1, A2)

Victim: **Andrew Rudolph Bramwell**
Race: Black
Date: March 14, 1996
Shot and killed by police after allegedly pointing what appeared to be a gun. The police received a call that there was a man armed with a knife. They stated that they chased him by foot after he had run away from them. An autopsy indicated that Bramwell was shot in the back three times.

(*Toronto Star*, March 16, 1996: A3)

Victim: John Anderson Braithwaite

Race: White

Date: May 27, 1996

He was shot twice and killed after allegedly attempting to attack a Metro officer with a knife. The officer involved was investigating a drug store robbery in Toronto. The officer was later cleared of any wrong doing by the SIU.

(*Toronto Star*, November 21, 1996: A20)

Victim: **Wayne Rick Williams**

Race: Black

Date: June 11, 1996

He was shot four times by police after they received a call that a man was smashing the windows of parked cars with a crowbar. He was shot after he refused to drop a knife which he also had in his possession. The police allege that he made threatening gestures before they shot him. One of the officers involved was also involved in another fatal shooting incident in 1985 but was cleared of any wrong doing.

(*Toronto Star*, June 12, 1996: A2)

Victim: **Edmond Wai Hong Yu**

Race: Asian

Date: February 20, 1997

Shot and killed by a Metro officer on an empty bus during rush hour in the presence of a dozen witnesses. The officer fired after the man pulled out a shiny hammer from his coat. The police were answering a call made by the bus driver claiming that a man was assaulting a woman. It was later discovered that Wai Hong Yu was suffering from schizophrenia. Several of the witnesses stated that they believed the force used by police was excessive. The police were cleared of any wrong doing by the SIU.

(*Toronto Star*, February 22, 1997: A21)

Victim: **Hugh Dawson**

Race: Black

Date: March 30, 1997

He was shot six times and killed after allegedly attempting to disarm a police officer during a drug bust. The officers involved refused to cooperate with the SIU investigation. Witness statements contradicted those of the police. Witnesses later reported that the shooting incident began when an officer smashed the Dawson's car window with a firearm causing it to discharge. Another officer on the other side of the car was hit with glass fragments which led the police to fire at Dawson. Rick Shank, one of the officers, wasmalso involved involved in the shooting death of Ian Coley in 1993 for which he was cleared of any wrong-doing.

(*Toronto Star*, April 1, 1997:A1, A24)

Victim: **Unidentified**

Race: Unknown

Date: April 13, 1997

He was shot and killed following a robbery at a Chinese restaurant. The police alleged that they observed a fleeing youth outside the restaurant and chased him on foot. Two other men bolted from the restaurant and started shooting at police attempting to arrest the youth. The officers returned fire as the two men ran to their car and escaped. It was unclear whether or not the shooting victim was also armed.

(*Toronto Star*, April 15, 1997: A3)

Appendix Three

Use of Force Report—Province of Ontario

Use Of Force Report

(Check more than one box in each section, where appropriate)

Police Service	Location Code

Part A

Date (day/month/year)	Time Incident Commenced (24 hr)		Time Incident Terminated (24 hr)

☐ Individual Report	Length Of Service (years completed)	Rank	☐ Team Report	Type of Team	# of Police Officers Involved

Type Of Assignment
- ☐ General Patrol
- ☐ Foot Patrol
- ☐ Traffic
- ☐ Investigation
- ☐ Drugs
- ☐ Off-duty
- ☐ Other (specify)

Type Of Incident
- ☐ Robbery
- ☐ Break and Enter
- ☐ Domestic Disturbance
- ☐ Other Disturbance
- ☐ Traffic
- ☐ Suspicious Person
- ☐ Serious Injury
- ☐ Homicide
- ☐ Weapons Call
- ☐ Alarm
- ☐ Other (specify)

Police Presence At Time Of Incident
- ☐ Alone
- ☐ Police Assisted (specify #) _____

Attire
- ☐ Uniform ☐ Civilian Clothes

Number of Subject(s) Involved in Incident
- ☐ One ☐ Two ☐ Three ☐ Other (specify #) _____

Type Of Force Used (include all options used during incident & rank in sequence of use)

		Was Force Effective? Yes	No
Firearm - discharged	__	☐	☐
Firearm - pointed at person	__	☐	☐
Handgun- drawn	__	☐	☐
Aerosol Weapon	__	☐	☐
Impact Weapon - Hard	__	☐	☐
Impact Weapon - Soft	__	☐	☐
Empty Hand Techniques - Hard	__	☐	☐
Empty Hand Techniques - Soft	__	☐	☐
Other (specify)	__	☐	☐

Reason For Use Of Force
- ☐ Protect Self
- ☐ Protect Public
- ☐ Effect Arrest
- ☐ Prevent Commission of Offence
- ☐ Prevent Escape
- ☐ Accidental
- ☐ Destroy an Animal
- ☐ Other (specify)

Alternative Strategies Used (If Applicable)
- ☐ Verbal Interaction ☐ Cover
- ☐ Concealment ☐ Other (specify)

Type Of Firearm Used (If Applicable) / **No. Of Rounds Discharged** (If Applicable)
- ☐ Revolver __
- ☐ Semi-automatic __
- ☐ Rifle __
- ☐ Shotgun __
- ☐ Other (specify) __

Distance (Between you & subject at the time the decision was made to use force)
- ☐ Less than 2 metres
- ☐ 2 to 3 metres
- ☐ 3 to 5 metres
- ☐ 5 to 7 metres
- ☐ 7 to 10 metres
- ☐ Greater than 10 metres

Weapons Carried By Subject(s)

1	2	3	
☐	☐	☐	Unknown
☐	☐	☐	None
☐	☐	☐	Revolver
☐	☐	☐	Semi-automatic
☐	☐	☐	Rifle
☐	☐	☐	Shotgun
☐	☐	☐	Knife/Edged Weapon
☐	☐	☐	Baseball Bat/Club
☐	☐	☐	Other (specify)

Location Of Subject's Weapon (At time decision was made to use force)

1	2	3	
☐	☐	☐	In-hand
☐	☐	☐	At hand
☐	☐	☐	Concealed on person

Number of Rounds Fired By Subject(s) (If Applicable)

Total Number: _____

Location Of Incident

Outdoors
- ☐ Roadway
- ☐ Laneway
- ☐ Yard
- ☐ Park
- ☐ Rural
- ☐ Motor Vehicle
- ☐ Other (specify)

Indoors

Private Property
- ☐ House
- ☐ Apartment
- ☐ Hallway

Public Property
- ☐ Financial Institution
- ☐ Commercial Site
- ☐ Public Institution
- ☐ Other (specify)

Weather Conditions
- ☐ Clear
- ☐ Sunny
- ☐ Cloudy
- ☐ Rain
- ☐ Snow/sleet
- ☐ Fog
- ☐ Other (specify)

Lighting Conditions
- ☐ Daylight
- ☐ Dusk
- ☐ Dark
- ☐ Good Artificial Light
- ☐ Poor Artificial Light
- ☐ Other (specify)

Person Injured / **Medical Attention Required** / **Nature Of Injuries**

Person Injured	Medical Attention Required Yes	No	Minor	Serious	Fatal	Unknown
1. Self	☐	☐	☐	☐		
2. Other Police Officer	☐	☐	☐	☐		
3. Subject	☐	☐	☐	☐	☐	☐
4. Third Party	☐	☐	☐	☐	☐	☐

Narrative: (If no occurrence report - Do not include personal names or information.)

If more space is required please continue on back of form.

Reviewed by Supervisor ☐ Yes ☐ No	Reviewed by Training Analyst ☐ Yes ☐ No	Recommended Post Traumatic Incident Counselling ☐ Yes ☐ No	Recommended Other Training ☐ Yes ☐ No	Date (day/month/year)

Part B

Officer Involved (name, rank & badge #)

Date of last use of force refresher training	Would you like to participate in an interview with a training sergeant/analyst to discuss this incident and/or use of force training? ☐ Yes ☐ No

Additional training recommended by: ☐ training analyst ☐ supervisor	Type of training recommended:

Appendix Four

Quebec Code of Police Ethics

2.2.2 Répartition des citations selon les articles du code de déontologie 1992-1993

Article	Description	%	%
5	Manque de confiance et de considération dans l'exercice de ses fonctions	21,0 %	2,8 %
5 - 1º	Langage blasphématoire et injurieux		7,0 %
5 - 2º	Omission ou refus de s'identifier		4,4 %
5 - 3º	Omission de porter une marque d'identification		—
5 - 4º	Propos injurieux (race, sexe, etc.)		2,4 %
5 - 5º	Manque de respect et de politesse		4,4 %
6	Abus d'autorité	55,1 %	18,6 %
6 - 1º	Utilisation d'une force plus grande que celle nécessaire		18,6 %
6 - 2º	Menaces, intimidation, harcèlement		11,5 %
6 - 3º	Fausse accusation		2,0 %
6 - 4º	Tenter d'obtenir une déclaration		1,6 %
6 - 5º	Détention illégale d'une personne qui n'est pas en état d'arrestation		2,8 %
7	Non-respect de la loi et de la justice	12,7 %	11,0 %
7 - 1º	Entrave à la justice		1,2 %
7 - 2º	Dissimulation d'une preuve		0,5 %
8	Manque de probité	4,8 %	0,8 %
8 - 1º	Dommage à un bien appartenant à autrui		1,6 %
8 - 2º	Disposition illégale d'un bien		0,4 %
8 - 3º	Présentation d'un rapport faux ou inexact		2,0 %
9	Conflit d'intérêt	0,4 %	0,4 %
9 - 1º	Acceptation d'une récompense ou d'un avantage		—
9 - 2º	Offre d'une récompense ou d'un avantage		—
9 - 3º	Recommandation d'un procureur en particulier		—
9 - 4º	Vente de publicité		—
10	Non-respect des droits de la personne	2,0 %	—
10 - 1º	Distribution d'alcool et de drogue		—
10 - 2º	Négligence à l'égard de la santé et de la sécurité		1,6 %
10 - 3º	Obtention d'un avantage indu pour une personne placée sous sa garde		—
10 - 4º	Fouille d'une personne de sexe opposé		—
10 - 5º	Ingérence dans les communications d'un procureur		0,4 %
10 - 6º	Brutalité envers une personne placée sous sa garde		—
10 - 7º	Incarcération inappropriée envers un mineur ou une personne du sexe opposé		—
11	Imprudence dans l'utilisation d'une arme ou d'une pièce d'équipement	4,0 %	2,8 %
11 - 1º	Utilisation d'une arme sans justification		1,2 %

Notes to Chapter One

[1] Robert Reiner, *The Politics of the Police* (Sussex: Wheatsheaf Books, 1985), pp. 20.

[2] Ibid., pp. 22.

[3] Ibid., pp. 21.

[4] Susie Bernstein, *The Iron Fist and the Velvet Glove* (California: Garrett Press, 1975), pp. 20.

[5] Ibid., pp. 22.

[6] Ibid., pp. 23-24.

[7] Caroline and Lorne Brown, *An Unauthorized History of the RCMP* (Canada: James Lorimer & Company, 1978), pps. 11-12.

[8] Ibid., pp. 22.

[9] Maggie Siggins, *Riel: A Life of Revolution* (Canada: Harper Perennial, 1994), pp. 445.

[10] Ian Taylor, "Martyrdom and Surveillance: Ideological and Social Practices of the Police in the 1980's", *Crime and Social Justice*, no. 26, 1986, pp. 61.

[11] Peter Manning, "Violence and the Police Role", *Annals.*, 452, 1980, pp. 136.

[12] William Waegal, "How to Justify the Use of Deadly Force", *Social Problems*, Vol. 32, 1984, pp. 150.

[13] Anton Gustin, "A Police Officer Reacts", *Journal of Social Issues*, Vol. 31, 1975, pp. 213.

[14] Steven Box and Ken Russel, "The Politics of Discredibility: Disarming Complaints Against the Police" in *Sociological Review*, 23 (2), pp. 315.

William Waegal, "How to Justify the Use of Deadly Force", *Social Problems*, Vol. 32, 1984, pp. 148.

Peter Manning, "Violence and the Police Role", *Annals.*, 452, 1980, pp. 136.

[15] Ibid., pp. 332.

[16] Anton Gustin, "A Police Officer Reacts", *Journal of Social Issues*, Vol. 31, 1975, pp. 214.

[17] Duncan Chappel and Linda Graham, *Police Use of Deadly Force in Canada* (Toronto: University of Toronto, 1985), pp. 102.

Notes to Chapter Two

[1] Frank Harrison, "Orwell and Anarchy in 1984" in *1984 and After* (Montreal: Black Rose Books, 1984), pps. 144-47.

[2] Stanley Cohen, *Visions of Social Control* (Cambridge: Polity Press, 1985), pp. 275.

[3] Attorney General of Canada, *Martin's Annual Criminal Code 1995*, (Toronto: Canada Law Books), Chap. C-34.

[4] Supreme Court Reports, "R. v. Storrey", [1990] Vol. 1, pp. 241.

[5] Attorney General of Canada, *Martin's Annual Criminal Code 1995*, (Toronto: Canada Law Books), Chap. C-34.

[6] Attorney General of Canada, *Martin's Annual Criminal Code 1995: First Supplement, Amendments*, (Toronto: Canada law Books), SUPP. 3.

[7] Andrew Duffy, "Ottawa Must Amend Police Gun Law, Report Says", *Toronto Star*, Feb. 21, 1992, pp. A7.

[8] Attorney General of Canada, *Martin's Annual Criminal Code 1995*, (Toronto: Canada Law Books), Chap. C-34.

[9] Ibid.

[10] Brian Grosman, *Police Command: Decisions and Discretion* (Toronto: Macmillan Company of Canada Ltd., 1975).

Carl Klockars, *The Idea of Police* (California: Sage Publications, 1985).

[11] Richard Kinsey and Jock Young, "Police Autonomy and the Politics of Discretion" in *Policing the Riots* (London: Junction Bookd Ltd., 1982), pp. 121.

Notes to Chapter Three

[1] Denis Chibnall, "Press Ideology: The Politics of Professionalism" in *Law and Order News*, 1977, pp. 12.

[2] John Fiske, *Reading the Popular* (Boston: Unwin Hyman, 1989), pp. 149.

[3] Ibid., pp. 169.

[4] Richard Ericson et. al., *Representing Order: Crime, Law, and Justice in the news Media* (Toronto: University of Toronto Press, 1991), pp. 165.

[5] Stuart Hall and C. Critcher, "The Social Production of News", *Policing the Crisis* (London: Macmillan, 1978), pp. 59.

[6] Stuart Hall and C. Critcher, "The Social Production of News", *Policing the Crisis* (London: Macmillan, 1978), pp. 56.

Denis Chibnall, "Press Ideology: The Politics of Professionalism" in *Law and Order News*, 1977, pp. 19.

[7] Richard Ericson et. al., *Representing Order: Crime, Law, and Justice in the news Media* (Toronto: University of Toronto Press, 1991), pp. 10.

[8] Ibid., pp. 12.

[9] Noam Chomsky, *The Chomsky Reader* (New York: Pantheon Books, 1987), pps. xi-xiii.

[10] Noam Chomsky, *Radical Priorities* (Montreal: Black Rose Books, 1981), pp. 12.

[11] Stuart Hall and C. Critcher, "The Social Production of News", *Policing the Crisis* (London: Macmillan, 1978), pps. 66-67.

[12] Mark Fishman, "Crime Waves as Ideology", *Social Problems*, Vol. 25, 1978, pp. 531.

[13] Ibid., pp. 532.

[14] Richard Ericson et. al., *Representing Order: Crime, Law, and Justice in the news Media* (Toronto: University of Toronto Press, 1991), pp. 204.

[15] Ewart Walters, "Vicious Backlash", *The Spectrum*, Vol. 9, 1992, pp. 1.

[16] Ibid., pp. 1.

[17] Michelle Lalonde, "Duchesneau: I Was Too Harsh", *Montreal Gazette*, April 22, 1998, pp. A16.

[18] James Mennie, "No Charges In Suazo Case: Police Chief", *Montreal Gazette*, December 16, 1997, pp. A3.

[19] Albert Noel, "Cops Ignored Bleeding Suazo, Coroner Told", *Montreal Gazette*, February 21, 1996, pp. A3.

[20] Editorial, "Justice Done in Barnabé Verdict", *Montreal Gazette*, June 27, 1996, pp. B2.

NOTES TO CHAPTER FOUR

[1] Lincoln Depradine, "Police Guns Boom Again", *Share*, Vol. 15, 1993, pp. 1.

[2] Eldridge Cleaver, *Soul on Ice* (New York: Bantam Doubleday Dell Publishing, 1992), pp. 75.

[3] Statistics Canada, *Ethnic Origins: 1991 Census of Canada* (Ottawa: Industry, Science and Technology, 1993).

[4] Ibid.

[5] James Mennie, "Policeman Suspended After 19-Year Old Slain", *Montreal Gazette*, Nov. 12, 1987, pp. A1.

[6] Catherine Buckie, "Ethics Panel Probes Shooting By Police", *Montreal Gazette*, February, 26, 1991, pp. A5.

[7] Michael Doyle and James Mennie, "Witnesses Raise Questions After Man Shot Dead By Officer", *Montreal Gazette*, January 4, 1989, pp. A1.

Albert Noel, "Cops Accused of Coverups", *Montreal Gazette*, May 16, 1989, pp. A1.

[8] Albert Noel and Jack Todd, "Man Killed By Police No Threat: Witness", *Montreal Gazette*, April 10, 1990, pp. A1, A2.

[9] Geoff Baker, "Police Officer gets 45 Days For High-Speed Death", *Montreal Gazette*, February 4, 95, pp. A1.

[10] Mike King, "Shoplifter Shot Dead By Undercover Officer", *Montreal Gazette*, November 23, 1990, pp. A3.

Mike King, "MUC Cop Cleared In Fatal Shooting", *Montreal Gazette*, July 20, 1992, pp. A3.

[11] Tu Thanh Ha, Andy Riga and Bart Kasowski, "François Dies of His Wounds", *Montreal Gazette*, July 9, 1991, pp. A1.

Albert Noel, "2 Cops Suspended For Abusing Authority In François Case", *Montreal Gazette*, September 15, 1994, pp. A3.

James Mennie, "François Inquest Reveals a Litany of Foulups", *Montreal*

Gazette, October 28, 1991, pp. A3, A4.

[12] Eddie Collister and James Mennie, "Car-Theft Suspect Shot Dead After Smashup Chase", *Montreal Gazette*, November 5, 1991, pp. A1, A2.

[13] Eddie Collister, "Black Man Dies In Scuffle With Police", *Montreal Gazette*, November 15, 1991, pp. A1, A2.

[14] Editorial, "Peaceable Montreal?", *Montreal Gazette*, January 5, 1993, pp. B2.

Michelle Lalonde, "Police Shot Kelly In the Back: Coroner", *Montreal Gazette*, January 5, 1993, pp. A1, A2.

[15] Alan Hustak, "Man Dies In Scuffle With SWAT Team", *Montreal Gazette*, March 7, 1993, pp. A3.

[16] Cal Millar and Don Dutton, "Shooting of Man Justified, Police Investigators Say", *Toronto Star*, October 19, 87, pp. A19.

[17] Nicholas Pron, "Injuries Ruled Unrelated To Death", *Toronto Star*, July 12, 1988, pp. A9.

[18] Cal Millar and Nicholas Pron, "Family Demands Impartial Probe Into Fatal Police Shooting", *Toronto Star*, August 11, 1988, pp. A1.

Gail Swainson, "Quest For the Truth In Donaldson Shooting", *Toronto Star*, July 8, 1994, pp. A21.

[19] Farrel Crook, "Grieving Mother Prays Slain Son Will Get 'Justice'", *Toronto Star*, April 11, 1992, pp. A4.

[20] Jim Wilkes, "Teen Killed, 3 Hurt Fleeing Police", *Toronto Star*, November 5, 1989, pp. A3.

[21] Don Dutton, "Police To Probe Fatal Shooting of Restaurant Hold-up Suspect", *Toronto Star*, January 26, 1990, pp. A1.

[22] Cal Millar, "Man Killed By Police Officers After Shot Blanks From Replica Gun", *Toronto Star*, December 31, 1990, pp. A1, A6.

[23] John Duncanson, "Officer Charged In Death Of Man", *Toronto Star*, June 28, 1994, pp. A1.

[24] Kelly Toughill, "Black Man Shot Dead By Undercover Officer", *Toronto Star*, May 3, 1992, pp. A1, A6.

Paul Maloney, "View of Shooting Blocked, Lawyer Says", *Toronto Star*, April 23, 1993, pp. A6.

[25] Gail Swainson and Peter Edwards, "Police Shoot, Kill Man Weilding Bat", *Toronto Star*, August 10, 1992, pp. A1.

[26] Moira Welsh, "Knifewielding Man Is Slain By Police", *Toronto Star*, December 27, 1992, pp. A1.

Moira Welsh, "Legal Battle Looming In Police Shooting Probe", *Toronto Star*, December 30, 1992, pp. A1, A20.

[27] Philip Mascol, "Gunman Fired First, Sources Say", *Toronto Star*, April 21, 1993, pp. A1, also Philip Mascol, "Son's Death Forgotten By Jurors, Mom Says", *Toronto Star*, August 19, 1995, pp. A4.

[28] Bruce Shepard, "Plain Racism: The Reaction Against Black Immigration

to the Canadian Plains", in *Racism in Canada*, 1991, pp. 15.

[29] Kevin Davis, "Controlling Racial Discrimination in Policing", *University of Toronto Faculty of Law*, Vol. 51, 1993, pp. 192.

Paul Gordon, *Racism in the Police, Courts and Prisons* (London: Pluto Press Ltd., 1983), pp. 77.

[30] Philip Mascol, "Blacks Face Extra Layer of Policing, Inquest Told", *Toronto Star*, June 24, 1995, pp. A4.

[31] Philip Mascol, "Help Boost War on Black Crime, Jury Urged", *Toronto Star*, July 9, 1995, pp. A7.

NOTES TO CHAPTER FIVE

[1] James Mennie, "Policeman Suspended After 19-Year Old Slain", *Montreal Gazette*, Nov. 12, 1987, pp. A1.

[2] James Mennie, " Keeping Gosset on Suspension Damaging to Force: Union Head", *Montreal Gazette*, Mar. 5, 1988, pp. A3.

[3] Elloise Morin and James Mennie, "Suspended Officer in Trouble Before", *Montreal Gazette*, Nov. 13, 1987, pp. A1.

[4] Montreal (CP), "Mother of Teenager Shot in Escape Bid to Sue Officer, City", *Toronto Star*, Nov. 14, 1987, pp. A19.

[5] Elloise Morin and James Mennie, "Suspended Officer in Trouble Before", *Montreal Gazette*, Nov. 13, 1987, pp. A1.

[6] Ibid., pps. A1, A2.

[7] James Quig, "Don't Blame Entire Force for Griffin Killing, Chief Says", *Montreal Gazette*, Nov. 21, 1987, pp. B1.

[8] Susan Semenak and Nancy Wood, "Probe Police Racism", *Montreal Gazette*, Nov. 22, 1987, pps. A1, A2.

[9] Ibid., pp. A1.

[10] Rod MacDonnel, "Constable Will Face Trial in Griffin Slaying", *Montreal Gazette*, Dec. 23, 1987, pp. A1.

[11] Ibid., pp. A1.

[12] Canadian Criminal Cases, "Regina v. Gosset", Quebec Court of Appeal, 67 C.C.C., 1991, pp. 156.

[13] Ibid., pp. 167.

[14] Montreal (CP), "I Didn't Mean to Shoot, Constable Says", *Toronto Star*, Feb. 19, 1988, pp. A9.

[15] Canadian Criminal Cases, "Regina v. Gosset", Quebec Court of Appeal, 67 C.C.C., 1991, pp. 162.

[16] Rod MacDonnel, "Jury Deliberating in Officer's Manslaughter Charge", *Montreal Gazette*, Feb. 23, 1988, pp. A3.

[17] Canadian Criminal Cases, "Regina v. Gosset", Quebec Court of Appeal, 67 C.C.C., 1991, pps. 185-87.

[18] Ibid., pp. 163.

[19] Rod MacDonnel, "Jury Deliberating in Officer's Manslaughter Charge", *Montreal Gazette*, Feb. 23, 1988, pp. A3.

[20] Don MacPherson, "Gosset's Trial Leaves Doubts Hanging", *Montreal Gazette*, Feb. 27, 1988, pp. B3.

[21] Alexander Norris, "Slain Youth's Grieving Mother Asks Whether Police Are Above the Law", *Montreal Gazette*, Feb. 25, 1988, pp. A1.

[22] James Mennie, " Keeping Gosset on Suspension Damaging to Force: Union Head", *Montreal Gazette*, Mar. 5, 1988, pp. A3.

[23] Peggy Curran, "Better Judgment Than Rules Gosset Says", *Montreal Gazette*, Apr. 21, 1988, pp. A3.

[24] Ibid.

[25] James Mennie, "Inquiry Finds Gosset 'Negligent' Recommends He Be Dismissed", *Montreal Gazette*, June 10, 1988, pp. A1.

[26] James Mennie, "Gosset Fired From MUC Police Force", *Montreal Gazette*, July 9, 1988, pp. A1.

[27] Peggy Curran, "Slaying Sparked Drive to Improve Relations Between Police, Minorities", *Montreal Gazette*, Nov. 12, 1988, pp. A1.

[28] James Mennie, "Gosset Fired From MUC Police Force", *Montreal Gazette*, July 9, 1988, pp. A1.

[29] Peggy Curran, "Gosset Gets $12,000 From Fellow Officers", *Montreal Gazette*, Nov. 5, 1988, pp. A2.

[30] Lynn Moore, "Carnations, Candles mark Spot Where Griffin lay Dying", *Montreal Gazette*, Nov. 12, 1988, pp. A4.

[31] James Mennie, "Gosset Starts Final Appeal to Regain MUC Police Job", *Montreal Gazette*, Nov. 29, 1988, pp. A3.

[32] Marian Scott, "Griffin Caused His Own Death Gosset's Lawyer Tells Hearing", *Montreal Gazette*, June 16, 1989, pp. A1.

[33] Ibid., pp. A1.

[34] Catherine Buckie, "Gosset Reinstatement 'Absurd':MUC", *Montreal Gazette*, Sept. 12, 1989, pp. A3.

[35] Elizabeth Thompson, "Take Gosset Back, Arbitrator Orders Police", *Montreal Gazette*, Aug. 25, 1989, pp. A1.

[36] Elizabeth Thompson and Aaron Defrel, "Police Chiefs Sacrificing Gosset to Minorities: Officers", *Montreal Gazette*, Aug. 30, 1989, pp. A1.

[37] Elizabeth Thompson, "Gosset Seeking Early Retirement", *Montreal Gazette*, Nov. 17, 1989, pp. A3.

[38] James Mennie, "Gosset Acquited Second Time", *Montreal Gazette*, Apr. 9, 1991, pp. A5.

[39] Catherine Buckie, "Gosset Reinstatement 'Absurd':MUC", *Montreal Gazette*, Sept. 12, 1989, pp. A3.

[40] Ibid., pp. A3.

[41] Elizabeth Thompson and Tu Thanh Ha, "Griffin's Mother Awarded $14,795 In Damages", *Montreal Gazette*, July 21, 1990, pp. A2.

[42] Rod MacDonnel and James Mennie, "Crown to Launch Appeal of Gosset's Acquittal", *Montreal Gazette*, Mar. 1988, pp. A1.

[43] Rene Laurent and Mike King, "Black Leaders Call Gosset's New Trial the 'Best News'", *Montreal Gazette*, May 25, 1991, pp. A2.

[44] Dominion Law Reports, "Regina v. Gosset", Supreme Court of Canada, Sept. 9, 1993, pp. 693.

[45] James Mennie, "Gosset Acquited Second Time", *Montreal Gazette*, Apr. 9, 1991, pp. A5.

[46] Ibid., pp. A5.

[47] Albert Neremberg, "Officers Down", *The Hour*, June 29, 1995, pp. 4.

[48] Elizabeth Thompson, "I Lost Control of Police: Chief", *Montreal Gazette*, July 9, 1993, pp. A1.

[49] Albert Neremberg, "Officers Down", *The Hour*, June 29, 1995, pp. 6.

[50] Albert Noel, "Reports on Suazo Shooting Given to Police Brotherhood Before Officers' Superiors", *Montreal Gazette*, May 15, 1996, pp. A5.

[51] Albert Noel, "Cops Accused of Coverups", *Montreal Gazette*, May 16, 1996, pp. A8.

NOTES TO CHAPTER SIX

[1] Editorial, "Protest Police Shooting Deaths", *Share*, Jan. 7, 1993, pp. 8.

[2] Betsy Powell, "Osler Quits Special Police Probe Unit", *Toronto Star*, June 16, 1992, pp. A7.

[3] Moira Welsh, "Police Feel 'Hurt, Anger' Over Attacks on Integrity", *Toronto Star*, Sept. 20, 1992, pp. A10.

[4] Bob Brent, "Officer's Manslaughter Hearing Begins in Donaldson Shooting", *Toronto Star*, April 25, 1989, pp. A23.

[5] Stephen Lewis, *Lewis Report on Race Relations*. Ontario, 1992, pp. 12.

[6] Ibid., pp. 4.

[7] Peter Small, "Reports Condemn 'Race Bias' in Metro Officers", *Toronto Star*, Sept. 11, 1992, pp. A32.

[8] Cal Millar, "Suspect Unarmed When Shot By Police", *Toronto Star*, Dec. 5, 1991, pp. A1.

[9] Charles Lewis, "Police Conduct Under Scrutiny", *Ottawa Citizen*, Mar. 21, 1993, pp. A4.

[10] Matt Maychak, "Civilian Set to Head Probe of Police", *Toronto Star*, June 29, 1990, pp. A3.

[11] Matt Maychak, "Civilians Should Retain Power to Discipline Police, Rae Says", *Toronto Star*, June 15, 1988, pp. A17.

[12] Charles Lewis, "Police Conduct Under Scrutiny", *Ottawa Citizen*, Mar. 21, 1993, pp. A4.

[13] Dr. Odida Quamina, "Police Accountability—Again", *Share*, Jan. 7, 1993,

pp. 7.

[14] Editorial, "Protest Police Shooting Deaths", *Share*, Jan. 7, 1993, pp. 8.

[15] John Duncanson, "Officer Charged in Man's Shooting", *Toronto Star*, Jan. 30, 1992, pp. A3.

[16] Steven Lewis, *Lewis Report on Race Relations*, Ontario, 1992, pp. 9.

[17] Dr. Odida Quamina, "Police Accountability—Again", *Share*, Jan. 7, 1993, pp. 7.

[18] Attorney General of Canada, *Ninth Annual Report of the Office of the Public Commissioner*, 1990, pp. 1.

[19] Caroline Abraham, "The Shooting of Vincent Gardiner", *Ottawa Citizen*, Feb. 13, 1993, pp. B5.

[20] Caroline Abraham, "Policing the Police: Public Watchdog Seen as Waste of Time and Money", *Ottawa Citizen*, March 20, 1993, pps. A1, A2.

[21] Ibid., pp. A1.

[22] Ibid., pp. A2.

[23] Ministry of the Solicitor General, *Use of Force Reporting-Standards and Form* (Ontario: Policing Services Division, 1992).

[24] Ibid.

[25] Ibid.

[26] Steven Lewis, *Lewis Report on Race Relations*, Ontario, 1992, pp. 11.

[27] John Duncanson, "Police Chief on the Carpet Over Job Action By his Officers", *Toronto Star*, Oct. 13, 1992, pp. A4.

[28] Caroline Mallan and Andrew Duffy, "Metro Police Defy Chief in Protest of Gun Law", *Toronto Star*, Sept. 8, 1992, pp. A1.

[29] Jacques Bellemaire, "Enquête sur les relations entre les corps policiers et les minorités visibles et ethniques: Les recommandations", Commission des Droits de la Personne de Québec.

[30] Daniel Drolet, "Police Academy—Quebec", *Ottawa Citizen*, April, 1993, pp. A2.

[31] Ingrid Peritz, "Police Under Fire Once Again: Minority Groups See a 'Trigger-Happy' Force", *Montreal Gazette*, July 12, 1991, pp. A4.

[32] Sandro Contenta, "Angry Blacks Denounce Police", *Toronto Star*, July 7, 1991, pp. A2.

[33] Aaron Defrel, "Man Shot by Police Cop Assault: Black Community Leaders Denounce MUC as Trigger-Happy", *Montreal Gazette*, Feb. 25, 1993, pp. A3.

[34] Sandro Contenta, "Black Man Shot By Police in Bungled Case", *Toronto Star*, July 6, 1991, pp. A2.

[35] Malouf, Albert, *The Malouf Report*, Gouvernement du Québec.

[36] Alexander Norris, "Let Civilians Investigate Police Shootings: Coroner", *Montreal Gazette*, May 4, 1993, pp. A1.

[37] Ibid., pp. A1.

[38] Ibid., pp. A1.

[39] Ibid., pp. A1.

[40] Lincoln Depradine, "Police Guns Boom Again", *Share*, Vol. 15, 1993, pp. 1.

[41] Alexander Norris, "Let Civilians Investigate Police Shootings: Coroner", *Montreal Gazette*, May 4, 1993, pp. A1.

[42] Noel, Albert, "Cops Accused of Coverups", *Montreal Gazette*, May 16, pp. A1.

[43] Ibid., pp. A8.

[44] James Mennie, "François's Death Might Lead to Public Inquiry: Decision Now Up to Coroner's Office", *Montreal Gazette*, July 20, 1991, pp. A3.

[45] Eddie Collister, "Leslie Fired First Shot, Coroner Rules", *Montreal Gazette*, Aug. 7, 1990, pp. A3.

[46] Montreal (CP), "Inqueest Called Into Shooting of Black man", *Toronto Star*, July 26, 1991, pp. A13.

[47] Gouvernement du Quebec, *Comité de Deontologie Policière: Rapport Annuel 1992-93* (Québec: Les Publications du Québec).

[48] Ibid., pp. 15.

[49] Ibid., pp. 16.

[50] Ibid., pp. 19.

[51] Ibid., pp. 18.

[52] Editor, "The Penalty Fits the Offence: Police Who Use Power for Own Ends Should Be Fired", *Montreal Gazette*, Feb. 18, 1993, pp. B2.

[53] Le programme d'accèss a l'égalité de S.P.C.U.M., *Le Respecte de la Différence: Bilan des réalisations*, MUC police, 1993, pps. 10-11.

NOTES TO CHAPTER SEVEN

[1] Stanley Cohen, *Visions of Social Control* (Cambridge: Polity Press, 1985), pp. 236.

[2] Thomas Mathiesen, "The Politics of Abolition", CC, 10:1, 1986, pp. 81.

[3] Maeve McMahon and Richard Ericson, "Reforming the Police and Policing Reform", in *State Control: Criminal Justice Politics in Canada*, 1987, pps. 39-40.

[4] Ibid., pp. 42.

[5] Ibid., pp. 44.

[6] Ibid., pp. 48.

[7] See Laureen Snider, "The Potential of the Criminal Justice System to Promote Feminist Concerns", *Studies in Law, Politics and Society*, 1990.

Selected Bibliography

Attorney General's Office *Ninth Annual Report of the Office of the Public Complaints Commissioner*, Public Complaints Commissioner (1990).

Attorney General of Canada. *Martin's Annual Criminal Code 1995.* Toronto: Canada Law Book, Inc. R.S.C. 1970, Chap. C-34 (1994a).

Attorney General of Canada. *Martin's Annual Criminal Code 1995: First Supplement, Amendments.* Toronto: Canada Law Book, Inc. (1994b).

Bellemaire, Jacques "Enquête sur les relations entre les corps policier et les minorités visibles et ethniques: Les recommandations," *Commission des Droits de la Personne de Québec.* Quebec (1988).

Bellemaire, Jacques, Alcindor, Maryse, Normandeau, André, Pelletier, Jean and Hedy *Enquête sur les relations entre les corps policier et les minorités visibles et ethniques: Les recommandations*, Final Report, Bibliothèque Nationale du Québec,(November 1988).

Bernstein, Susie et al. *The Iron Fist and the Velvet Glove: An Analysis of the U.S. Police.* Berkeley: Garrett Press, Inc., (1975).

Box, Steven and Ken Russel "The Politics of Discredibility: Disarming Complaints Against the Police", *Sociological Review.* 23 (2) (May, 1975): 315-46.

Brown, Caroline and Lorne Brown *An Unauthorized History of the RCMP.* Toronto: James Lorimer & Company(1978).

Canadian Criminal Cases "Regina v. Gosset", Quebec Court of Appeal, 67 C.C.C. (3d), (May 24, 1991) Pp. 156-187.

Chappel, Duncan and Linda P. Graham *Police Use of Deadly Force in Canada.* Toronto: University of Toronto Press, (1985).

Chibnall, Denis "Press Ideology: The Politics of Professionalism" in *Law and Order News*, (1977), Pp. 11-45.

Chomsky, Noam *Radical Priorities.* Montreal: Black Rose Books, Inc., (1981).

Chomsky, Noam *The Chomsky Reader.* New York: Pantheon Books, Inc., (1987).

Cleaver, Eldridge *Soul on Ice.* New York: Bantam Doubleday Dell Publishing Group, Inc., (1992).

Cohen, Stanley *Visions of Social Control.* Cambridge: Polity Press, (1985).

Davis, Kevin "Controlling Racial Discrimination in Policing: A Discussion

Paper", *University of Toronto Faculty of Law Review*. Vol. 51, Spring, 1993, Pp. 179-203.

Depradine, Lincoln "Police Guns Boom Again", *Share*, Toronto. Vol. 15, No. 8, (Jan 7, 1993):1.

Dominion Law Reports "Regina v. Gosset", Supreme Court of Canada, Court File No. 22523, 105 D.L.R. (4th), September 9,1993, Pp. 681-699.

Ericson, Richard V., Banarek, Patricia M. and Janet B.L. Chan, *Representing Order: Crime, Law, and Justice in the News Media*. Toronto: University of Toronto Press, (1991).

Fishman, Mark "Crime Waves as Ideology" *Social Problems*, Vol. 25, No. 5, (1978), Pp. 531-543.

Fiske, John *Reading the Popular*. Boston: Unwin Hyman, Inc, (1989).

Franklin, H. Bruce *Prison Literature in America: The Victim as Criminal and Artist*. New York: Oxford University Press, Inc. (1989).

Gordon, Paul *Racism in the Police, Courts and Prisons*. London: Pluto Press (1983).

Gouvernement du Quebec *Comité de Deontologie Policiere: Rapport Annuel 1992-1993*. Quebec: Les Publications du Québec, (1993).

Grosman, Brian *Police Command: Decisions and Discretion*. Toronto: Macmillan Company of Canada Ltd., (1975).

Gustin, Anton "A Police Officer Reacts", *Journal of Social Issues*. Vol. 31, No. 1, (1975). Pp. 211-215.

Hall, Stuart and C. Critcher "The Social Production of News," *Policing the Crisis*. London: Macmillan. (1978) Pp. 53-406. Harrison, Frank "Orwell and Anarchy in 1984", in M. Hewitt and D. Roussopoulos (eds.), *1984 and After*. Montreal: Black Rose Books Ltd, (1984), Pp. 143-170.

Kinsey, Richard and Jock Young "Police Autonomy and the Politics of Discretion" in D. Cowell, T. Jones and J. Young (eds.), *Policing the Riots*, London: Junction Books, Ltd. (1982) 118-134.

Klockars, Carl *The Idea of Police*. California: Sage Publications (1985).

Malouf, Albert H. *The Malouf Report*. Gouvernement du Québec, Cabinet du Ministre de la Securité Publique (1992).

Manning, Peter "Violence and the Police Role", *Annals.*, AAPSS, 452, (November, 1980). pp. 135-144.

McMahon, Maeve W. and Richard V. Ericson "Reforming the Police and

Policing Reform", in R.S. Ratner and J. McMullan (eds.) Pp. 38-68. *State Control: Criminal Justice Politics in Canada* (1987).

Ministry of the Solicitor General *Use of Force Reporting-Standards and Form*. Ontario: Policing Services Division (1992).

Reiner, Robert *The Politics of the Police*. Sussex: Wheatsheaf Books, (1985).

Scott, Nolvert P. Jr. "The Black Peoples of Canada" in D. G. Baker (Ed.), *Politics of Race*, 143-162 (1975).

Shadd, Adrienne "Institutionalized Racism and Canadian History: Notes of a Black Canadian" in O. McKague (Ed.), *Racism in Canada*, (1991) pps.1-14.

Shepard, R. Bruce "Plain Racism: The Reaction Against Black Immigration To the Canadian Plains" in O. McKague (Ed.) *Racism in Canada*, (1991) 15-31.

Siggins, Maggie *Riel: A Life of Revolution*. Canada: Harper Perennial (1994).

Snider, Laureen "The Potential of the Criminal Justice System To Promote Feminist Concerns", *Studies in Law, Politics and Society*, (1990), 10:143-172.

Statistics Canada *Ethnic Origins: 1991 Census of Canada*. Ottawa: Industry, Science and Technology. Catalogue number 93-315, (1993).

Supreme Court Reports "R. v. Storrey", [1990] Vol. 1, (1990).

Taylor, Ian "Martyrdom and Surveillance: Ideological and Social Practices of the Police in the 1980's", *Crime and Social Justice*, (1986) No. 26. Pps. 60-78.

Waegal, William B. "How to Justify the Use of Deadly Force", *Social Problems*. Vol. 32, No. 2, (December, 1984) Pps. 144-155.

Walters, Ewart "Vicious Backlash", *The Spectrum*, Toronto. Vol. 9, No. 9, (August 4, 1992) Pp. 1.

Walters, Ewart "Tell the Children the Truth." *The Spectrum*, Vol. 9, No. 9, (August 4, 1992) Pps. 5-6.

Yeboah, Samuel Kennedy *The Ideology of Racism*. London: Hansib Publishing (1988).